THE LISTENING LEADER

THE LISTENING LEADER

Powerful New Strategies for Becoming an Influential Communicator

Richard M. Harris

Westport, Connecticut
London

Library of Congress Cataloging-in-Publication Data

Harris, Richard M., 1938–
    The listening leader : powerful new strategies for becoming an influential
communicator / Richard M. Harris.
        p. cm.
    Includes bibliographical references and index.
    ISBN 0-275-98983-6 (alk. paper)
    1. Communication in management   2. Listening.   3. Business communication.
4. Leadership.   I. Title.
    HD30.3.H3718 2006
    658.4'5—dc22   2006001240

British Library Cataloguing in Publication Data is available.

Library of Congress Catalog Card Number: 2006001240
ISBN: 0-275-98983-6

First published in 2006

Praeger Publishers, 88 Post Road West, Westport, CT 06881
An imprint of Greenwood Publishing Group, Inc.
www.praeger.com

Printed in the United States of America

The paper used in this book complies with the
Permanent Paper Standard issued by the National
Information Standards Organization (Z39.48-1984).

10   9   8   7   6   5   4   3   2   1

To my dear mother, Isabelle W. Harris, of blessed memory. I am a bene-ficary of her life-long love of words and fascination with their meanings. A sensitive and accomplished writer, her letters, articles, poems, and short stories frequently appeared in local newspapers and magazines. Yet she never realized seeing her *magnum opus*—her novel-length manuscript—in published form. It is in her memory that I dedicate this book.

Contents

Preface

In today's complex, fast-paced, and high-intensity organizations, effective communication is paramount. But all too often, messages are misinterpreted, ignored, or missed altogether—stifling creativity, morale, collaboration, and even basic achievement of goals. An all-too-common confession I hear is "I've never been a good listener. My problem is, I'm always...(impatient, distracted, multitasking)." This self-assessment may be accurate, but it's not helpful. These and similar self-flagellating thoughts only keep one frustratingly at ground zero and beg the questions: Why? What can I do about it? What's really in it for me if I change?

Indeed, much information seems to slip through whatever nets we are using at the moment to trawl the conversation. We waste a fair amount of time doing damage control around misunderstanding. And too many of us miss valuable opportunities to get the information we need quickly and accurately, to accomplish a variety of interpersonal goals and save precious time. Heightened stress and frustration are often the bitter fruits of our hapless efforts. And I believe the poor state of knowledge of and practice in listening contributes to some of these bad outcomes.

The Listening Leader is about improving communication by focusing on listening and, in the process, developing more effective leadership skills throughout an organization. It explores ways in which managers and front-line employees alike can elevate listening to the level of *influence* itself—to maximize conversational value and relationships through response and feedback.

Influence hardly seems the proper word to describe listening. But, what takes listening out of the ordinary is the determination to go *beyond private understanding*, to interact with the speaker in order to share a deeper level of mutual understanding and rapport. Inward-looking listeners must expand their vision if they are to help themselves and others excel. Even in this age of technology—or perhaps especially now—feedback remains the social currency that secures the bond between speaker and listener. More than this, feedback strengthens focus, reduces stress, and even has motivational value.

The Listening Leader integrates insights from management and psychology and offers practical techniques for overcoming common barriers to effective listening. With tips for keeping listening sharp and advice for boosting memory and recall, the book provides readers with the tools to engage in much more productive dialogue with colleagues, supervisors, employees, customers, and even those relationships beyond work.

My own perspective on these complex issues has developed over the past thirty years as a result of my work as a professional trainer in contact with executives, managers, engineers, scientists, and salespeople in many different types of settings. The greatest lesson that I have learned is that what differs most from situation to situation, from person to person, is not the nature of the distraction, but the individual's way of processing a message and responding to it.

This book, then, has two aims. First, to provide a broader and deeper understanding of listening and our role in it: historical, cultural, and personal factors that inhibit its practice and underlying process dynamics that ensure its greater success. Second, to illuminate the influencing aspect of listening and the tools available (steps we can take) to energize others, to guide and motivate them to more authentically communicate. In this way, conversation is more meaningful, the tone more satisfying. All parties get more out of the encounter. I hope, in the process, to excite your imagination and to inspire you to join others in rejuvenating your resolve to rethink, to change, to move in this more positive direction, and to grow.

Turning listening from a passive, compliant role into an active, influential one contributes to more dynamic, trusting, and profitable relationships through which everyone benefits. So set yourself this realistic goal today: to learn how to make conversations more efficient and productive, and to engender more mutual satisfaction, by becoming—and being recognized as—a true *listening leader*.

Acknowledgments

I am sure many of us have flipped through a book and taken only bare notice of the acknowledgments page. Perhaps we have seen this as some dutiful gesture that the author is obliged to include in his or her work. (I know I have been guilty of this.) But truthfully, few come by their accomplishments solely through their own efforts. We may not always be able to trace the source of our ideas, formulations, or even inspiration, but there are other partners whose influence informs our creations and enables us to bring them to fruition. This is certainly true in my case.

And so, far from merely conforming to some literarily correct doctrine, I welcome this opportunity to acknowledge a true debt of gratitude first of all to John Willig, my superbly communicative and supportive agent—a rare find. It was he who, from the very beginning, believed in me and my project, and whose keen perception, rich experience, and expert guidance kept me on track throughout the proposal process—and always with a buoyant sense of humor.

I would like to thank Nick Philipson, my editor, for his tremendous support and assistance in completing this book. Not only did he freely share his contagious enthusiasm and genuine encouragement, but he was also always there to suggest what really mattered in my manuscript.

I'd also like to thank the many men and women who shared their personal listening experiences and feedback with me. They truly helped me grow in this regard. And I owe a special debt of gratitude to my wife, Estelle, for teaching me about some aspects of listening that I had not fully appreciated and for helpfully hearing me out about my favored phrasings and commenting with sometimes not so gentle—but always welcome—objectivity on my latest humble offerings.

And finally, I would like to thank my children, friends, and acquaintances—helpful parties all—who have aided this project more than they know by letting me run my latest ideas by them, whether a telling example, an apt phrase or analogy, or perhaps a preferred choice of title. In the process, they helped refine my sense of what effective listening is really all about.

PART 1

Why Listen?

CHAPTER 1

Approaching Listening

We take listening—our own as well as that of others—very much for granted. Paying attention to what someone is telling us, day in and day out, is so routine and commonplace that it strikes us as almost instinctive (like breathing). This seems natural enough. After all, listening is merely a practical tool for collecting a speaker's information and getting his or her meaning. Like speech itself, we focus not on the act but on the goal.

Thinking About Listening

Accordingly, the *experience of listening* remains on the edge of our awareness, leaving us largely unconscious of its presence and oblivious to its process. As a result, many of us have at best an intellectual appreciation of listening, but are dulled to its qualities. Like cancer, we know it in the abstract and from a distance. (It is only when we—or someone close to us—personally experiences the ravages of this disease that it suddenly bears in on us with immediate impact and somehow becomes real.)

So it is with listening. Listening's reality pops into awareness only when someone might say, accusingly, "You're not listening"; or when you sense that another is not giving you her full attention; or on those rare occasions when you catch yourself drifting.

But what is listening, really? How can we gain some perspective on the nature of this subtle, slippery, and seemingly haphazard activity? We can bring it into sharper focus and get a handle on it by reflecting on it.

Observations and Questions

Let's begin with a few important observations and orienting questions. First: *Are hearing and listening the same thing?* Most people know that they are not. But how are they different? This distinction is important for us. We hear by chance—on the chance that there is enough energy (sound) in the immediate environment to stimulate the ear. It is a solitary, isolated, individual act—a passive process, having little to do with understanding. Listening, on the other hand, is something we do by *choice*. We decide whether, when, and to what (or whom) we will listen. Here, the mind is engaged in its orientation toward meaning: We are mentally involved as we take in information, interpret it, evaluate it, and prioritize it. In short, when we listen, we're *thinking*.

But concentration is fickle and fleeting, and some of us are highly distractable. There are those who believe that our most precious ability, the knack of creation, is also our most fleeting resource. If so, the ability to fully concentrate—and sustain it over the course of a conversation—is surely a close second. Listening is a situation that needs constant tending.

How do we commonly perceive the roles of speaker and listener? In the popular mind, we are most active when we are engaged in talking. According to this view, we assert and fulfill ourselves in the act of verbalizing. Speech is power, or so the conventional wisdom goes. Seen this way, listening would appear to be a passive, compliant role in which the receiver must wait before responding, until the speaker either asks a question or yields the speaking turn (power base). Now, if this were indeed true—and it's a big *if*—why would anyone want to listen? The listener seems, at best, to be assigned a powerless, inactive, accompanying role in conversation as opposed to the speaker's strong, active, and dominant one. (Is this perhaps, in part, why the typical listener tends to look inward at the rational and emotional landscape of his or her own psyche rather than outward at the conversation that involves him or her?)

Listening is complex and nuanced. It is imbued with personal and emotional concerns. Major difficulties touch our lives such as those concerning health, employment, deadlines, personal goals, relationship issues, ultimate meaning, work-related matters ... the accumulated clutter of every day and of a lifetime. There are also issues of ego and respect.

When we reflect on listening, *how do we properly conceive of and realize it*? We probably see it more as an art than a craft, a personal disposition rather than an affecting presence. Yet, you know how affirming it feels to be truly listened to. Although it doesn't happen that often, when it does, you sit there pleasantly jolted, grateful, and freely expressive, and think, "Why can't more conversations be like this?"

But *what is the persuasive power of efficient, sensitive listening*? As the essayist and novelist Susan Sontag has observed: "It's the response that comes when a listener's feedback so spontaneously and completely complements your communication that you find yourself truly feeling fully understood, even when you want to regain your more reserved posture. The focus tightens, the guard goes down. And there is somehow the sense that ordinary conversation has been transformed into real *dialogue*." To be sure, response is a gift a listener can lavish or withhold.

Practical Value

Someone once said, "We minimize the value of a darned good conversation." What is that value? It's just being polite, paying another respect, one might say. But listening, especially in business, is more than altruism, more than a humanitarian gesture; and the stakes of course are much higher. Subpar listening is more than social indiscretion; it can be extremely costly. Most people don't need to be reminded of the billions of dollars wasted yearly in lost time and productivity in sales, in one-to-one conversations, conference calls, meetings, and interviews.

Superior listening for Jill—who sells pharmaceuticals for a major company and spends the bulk of her time on the road visiting and communicating with clients—can mean a better chance of boosting sales. For Brian—a construction engineer whose busy job has him constantly communicating with suppliers, subcontractors, and inspectors, while assigning and monitoring tasks throughout the day—it means a way of achieving trustful working relationships. For Mark—a CEO of a major electronics corporation, whose global travels and oversight of telecommunications and semiconductor projects require him to be constantly available to customers, employees, and vendors—it can be a means of gaining greater credibility and smoother operations. And for Mary—an information technology administrator—more effective listening helps her answer questions and provide needed, on-the-mark solutions to user groups utilizing a new software program. Just as Jill, Brian, Mark, and Mary share—with us—the desire to meet personal goals and corporate objectives, they are also not alone in needing sharper listening awareness, a different way of thinking, and better techniques to achieve them.

When we listen, we also learn and retain more; we sell more; and we earn the respect, friendship, and cooperation of others. People are more willing to share with us their true thoughts and feelings because they sense that we genuinely care. With less frustration and conflict, we can save time, accomplish goals more easily, make our jobs more satisfying, and life becomes more rewarding.

Although our individual purposes may vary, we all share the same goal: to succeed at one of the most mentally demanding, socially challenging, and emotionally stressful tasks in our life—*being a listener in a conversation.*

Hindering Habits

The listening problem or problems need to be spelled out if we are to find a solution. One of the problems listening poses at times for all of us is *combating our own inattentiveness.* Not all talk will engage our attention and keep it. Besides, many loose ideas float around in our minds. Our listening is often the casualty of mental stress, particularly when under the strain of self-interest, defensiveness, fatigue, or strong emotion. Or we may simply lack interest. A frequent admission I hear is, "I have a tendency to think about other things I have to do when others are talking". Concentration becomes weak and then dissipates, like smoke. How can we strengthen our resisting power to distraction?

What about the past and how it exerts a persistent grip on the present? I sometimes wonder how many of us are aware of this ever-present background that influences the ways we hear and perceive others.

Then, too, *much listening is rooted in impatience*—with the speaker, the message, or both. "I often assume too early that I know what a person means and jump to conclusions," a sales manager in one of my workshops once told me. With today's frenetic pace of business and even everyday living, many a listener is understandably put off by those who take too long to get to the point or those who go into too much detail. Paying attention to an unstimulating speaker may be the right thing to do, but how many of us can pull it off? Staying focused and feeling connected while being berated by an angry boss, customer, or colleague may be desirable, but do we know how to make it happen? Restless listeners lose the present while waiting for the future.

Yes, listening is a real cognitive workout. It is not somehow natural and easy but exceedingly difficult to achieve another's frame of reference. Neither is it a small accomplishment to govern our emotions, control our concentration, and skillfully relate to others. Few of us have acquired the knowledge and tools that facilitate listening to others. Yet, whether it means staying focused or keeping a rein on our emotions, it's something like quitting smoking: *If you learn about it, get encouragement, and come to grips with it, you can control it.*

Rewards

But let's face it. Most of us are motivated through incentives. What is the reward for working on improving the quality of conversations and the quality of relationships? Individually, when we help customers and coworkers satisfy their goals, we can more easily accomplish our own (helping others excel is a mark of true leadership). Say you're a sales manager whose job is to lead, teach, and coach your people. Knowing how to really listen can win their loyalty, reduce selling-time costs, and increase efficiencies (not to mention reduce the cost of turnover—lost sales, lost opportunity, and even lost customers). With listening team leaders like you, management can develop effective teams and team players. You and your colleagues thus distinguish yourselves as top performers who are seen as strong contributors to the organization's overall success. And companies can vault themselves to the top tier of leadership in their industry. Productivity can grow. Morale can thrive.

Some First Considerations

Unfortunately, few people engage in listening as a contact sport. I find this strikingly evident in the listening-leadership workshops that I facilitate for corporations. In these, listeners are videotaped in simulated one-on-one conversations with others in the group. This gives an extremely rare and even a first-time glimpse of someone actually performing in the listener's role. Because we largely lack the ability to see ourselves as others do—and also don't *hear* ourselves—participants quite often remark on how unexpressive and wooden they appear while listening.

I wonder how many of us have ever really observed a listener close up, in action. Probably very few. More likely, we have taken notice of speakers and how they present themselves. Conversation seems, by its nature, to be speaker focused and speaker driven.

As listeners we physically and visually orient ourselves toward the speaker. Our eyes scan the speaker's face and body, picking up expressive cues that help define the overall message and its meaning. But this focusing away from self leaves us with scant awareness of how our conversational companion perceives *us*, whether in groups or in one-to-one listening relationships.

Listener Presentation: An Example

How do listeners present in conversation? What behaviors do they exhibit? Let's imagine a face-to-face conversation taking place in an office on the second floor. Bob's boss has called him in to explain the company's new strategic marketing initiative and how it will affect Bob's job as marketing manager.

As his boss describes the nature and scope of the new venture, Bob is thinking ahead about the extra time this will require of him. It stresses him that he now has to rearrange priorities and take some people off other projects. He feels a twinge of angry resentment over not being involved in this decision and being given such short notice. We see Bob sitting there mute and unmoving, but agitated inside and weighed down by the burden of his emotions as he struggles to process what his boss is saying and to cope with its unsettling implications. Behind his stoic demeanor is a relentless activism as his mind silently accuses his boss of unfairness. Bob's defensive reaction is natural, but ineffective. Bob is unable to rebound as his boss continues to speak, his words now becoming faint background. The preoccupations of the two drift further apart. Bob draws deeper within himself instead of reaching out toward his partner. He holds himself aloof, unaware that, in his silence, he is more easily given to self-absorption and loss of focus. It would appear that Bob's impassive stance has less to do with his lack of understanding than with his self-distraction and reluctance to respond. What is there to say when the meaning is entirely clear and he hasn't been invited to express his feelings or opinion? Besides, he doesn't want to interrupt. We will return to this example later.

Bob is fairly typical of the average manager. He fails to see any way to control his mounting feelings, maintain focus, and engage his boss in a respectful and open give-and-take. Understandably absorbed in his personal dilemma, Bob gives little thought to how he could respond to his boss so as to make this conversation less uncomfortable for both of them.

Neither of them seems to be willing or to know how to open up honestly with the other.

We can all recognize this reality. Many of us face similar situations in our personal lives and on the job. Distracted by swerves of thought and the rising tide of our emotions, we search in vain for some way to get our brains to click back into gear. Many of us feel unable to cope with the stiff challenges such circumstances pose to our mental focus and listening composure, and therefore often shut down or lash out uncontrollably, overtaken by anger, frustration, anxiety, or fear. How can we stay focused, keep control of our emotions, and go the distance?

Listening Proactively

For supervisors to succeed today in an era of constant change, corporate restructuring, and complex challenges, we must recast our traditional role and self-image. As listeners, we must come to see ourselves, begin to act, and help others see us not as distant, listless receivers but as up-front motivators and active guides to those with whom we interact.

A great deal of listening is a reflexive reaction to something a speaker says or does. This unplanned, unconscious, knee-jerk inclination almost seems beyond our control. But this is not always so. True leaders demonstrate an ability to listen *proactively,* bringing to conversations a deliberate strategy, a design that keeps them ever alert to meaning and nuance, to how the speaker feels about what he or she is saying. They monitor themselves as well as their partners. Proactive listeners, through feeding back and questioning, *create* action, instead of just following it. This aspect of listening has been undervalued for too long.

Many years ago, when I expressed frustration with my own nervousness in public speaking, colleagues dismissed my concerns. "You'll get over it," they assured me. These unhelpful words, which have stuck with me ever since, betray an unthinking outlook that assumes that the first thing on a speaker's mind is not what to do, but how to cope. The "solution" lay less in a method than in the sentiment and resignation to the passage of time and to one's fate (reactive versus proactive).

The Accidental Listener

Many of us are also listeners by happenstance. We tend to give our attention only if others are focused, compelling speakers whose subject is of interest or relevance to us. Yes, perhaps, as in the words of a banking senior vice president and chief information officer in one of my training sessions, "There is nothing more enjoyable than listening to a gifted speaker." And as another participant, a supervisor of project planning, told me, "It takes a deliberate effort to concentrate on material that I am not responsible for." But in truth, few speakers and situations meet such high requirements. Although these attitudes may be intellectually attractive, they are ultimately cop-outs that put the full responsibility for our listening squarely on other people's shoulders. Let's admit it: there are times when managers simply must be able to dig out essential information even from a "weak signal." If we're going to make real progress in listening and influencing, we need to stop blaming speakers and start taking more responsibility for our own behavior. (Later in this book, we will see how feedback liberates listening from overdependence on interesting speakers.) Yet we need to have intelligent understanding, the tools, and confident execution to get the job done.

What does it take to be not just an average or even a good listener, but a great listener—a *listening leader*? What traits or characteristics must one possess? Over the course of the following chapters, we will move toward an intelligent, informed answer to this fundamental question and summarize essential listening-leadership qualities in the form of an acronym spelling the word **p-r-e-s-e-n-t** (as in fully present). This stands for listeners who **p**roactively **p**articipate, **r**eview, listen **e**mpathetically, sidestep **s**tar events, make an **e**ffort to pay attention, **n**eutralize snap judgments, and **t**enaciously track the speaker and the message (see Chapter 10).

For now, we can define an average listener as someone in conversation who drifts in and out of focus, gets only the general gist of the speaker's message, and offers minimal feedback (like our friend, Bob, in the earlier example).

Clearly, not many in the manager's role today have the luxury of leisurely contemplation. A manager or supervisor must get the information—and cooperation—he or she needs to make smart decisions, take required action, and get on with business. Therefore, it is crucial for managers to have a correct perspective on listening, develop better technique, and through guided practice, lead more easily for best results.

Questions and Concerns

Like the hub of a wheel, the listening experience is at the center of numerous intersecting questions and concerns deserving of clear-eyed discussion, if not definitive answers. For example, managers in my workshops often ask: "How can I become a more patient listener?" "How can I stay focused or regain focus?" "What can or should I say in this particular situation?" "When should I interject?" They also express personal concern about such things as how to be less distractable, how to acknowledge that the message is getting through, what can be done to maintain emotional balance, what to listen for in conversation, how to read a speaker's true intent, and how to boost retention.

These are important and valid matters, yet what most supervisors and others don't seem to realize is the pivotal role feedback plays in conversation. They do not appreciate, for example, how creative responding can act as a propellant, spurring the conversation forward. Nor do they realize how feedback positively impacts focus, relationship, memory, both speaker and listener, and interpersonal goals. Finally, what it might mean to actually become an *influential* listener—and how to accomplish this—rarely makes their cherished wish list. Although many know that how an idea is presented will greatly influence how it is received, far fewer appreciate the opposite—*that the way a message is received will greatly influence its presentation.*

Before more fully examining these and other questions, we first need to consider more basic ones: What is the society-related backdrop to contemporary efforts to listen? What is the cultural soil in which listening would take root?

The Impact of Technology and Culture

With proliferating telecommunications technology and increasingly rapid access to global information in our digital age, there is much to applaud. But observers have also noted a disturbing downside: stress levels are climbing even as attention spans are growing shorter. This sober reality makes the manager's job as a listener (and as a speaker) even more daunting.

Yet, as some point out, another, perhaps subtler factor at work is the characteristic American virtue of autonomy. Our society and culture *arguably* prize autonomy and individuality above attachment and intimacy. As a professional trainer, I have often seen this unconscious value deeply embedded in the noncommunicative quality of much one-sided, unengaging talk and listening. This go-it-alone style also puts would-be influential managers at a serious disadvantage in their efforts to stay focused and feel connected.

The Listening Gap

To be sure, listening is an extremely hard road to travel today. So many things get in the way: deadlines, multitasking, personal worries, family concerns, exhaustion, stress, and boredom. Small wonder that average listening efficiency is only about 25 percent (based on studies conducted and reported by Ralph G. Nichols in *Are You Listening?*, 1967). But we don't have to settle for this percentage. We can narrow our losses and do much more than that. We can potentially guide our conversations toward more satisfying outcomes. All of us can function at a much higher level of listening quality and efficiency—and increase the transaction value per conversation—*by knowing how and practicing regularly.*

What accounts for such low performance? Many things contribute, but the major hurdles seem be the preference to talk, the reluctance to respond, mental clutter, judging, distraction, emotions, and defensiveness. We will turn to these in subsequent chapters.

Curbing the Tendency to Overtalk

You've seen them and may even have been one of their victims. They have a fetish for talking: the overzealous salesperson, the conversation-hogging colleague with no sense of holding back, as one should, so as not to smother, if not interrupt, you. They barrel along in overdrive, seemingly unaware or not caring that their conversational companion may be supersaturated, if not bored to tears.

The success of managers and sales professionals hinges not only on speaking confidently and compellingly but also on listening attentively and responsively. Influential listeners display this quality of leadership—and gain a loyal following—by respecting, motivating, and developing others who work with them.

Respect and loyalty belong to those who earn it. Underperformed listening compromises these virtues, and this negatively impacts our effectiveness in communicating, coaching and mentoring, appraising, motivating, and managing others.

Our better judgment tells us that there are times to talk and times to be quiet. Sometimes one can accomplish more through empathic silence, an acknowledging head nod or facial expression, or supportive inquiry. Therapists know that even the simplest 'hmmm,' or nod of the head, or 'Yes?' or silence (particularly silence) will steer the direction and content of a dialogue. Or listen in to the empathic responding of a colleague at work:

Worker: My wife just lost her mother … and her job right now is a little shaky.

Coworker: That must be hard on you. How are you managing? How is she taking it?

The Impulsive Speaker

Sadly, though, what we often hear in conversation is a speaker in love with the sound of his or her voice. But when we become too enamored of our own voices, it's hard to keep our minds on another's. The impulse to talk is almost always fired by ego. Many simply cannot wait to get on with talking, as if nature also abhors an unspoken moment. (A common concern heard in my listening workshops is how to avoid attempting to insinuate one's opinions or monopolizing the conversation when dialoguing.) Those in sales who have the solution to the customer's need and want to make it known—as well as managers who have the answer to the subordinate's problem—must learn to control this eagerly aggressive quality. Such individuals have a powerful appetite for dominating the conversation and determining its course. If they are not careful, they can be overwhelming and can cause the speaker to miss important elements in what others are saying. More than leaving a negative impression, *it may hamper one's motivation to take a desired action.* Often managers forget this in their dealings with subordinates, as do salespeople with buyers.

I remember telling an acquaintance about my experience addressing a singles group. Caught up in self-interest and the stimulation of relating this first-ever event in my life, it did not register with me when the woman said, "I have wide experience with that." I simply pushed on, saying somewhat dismissively, "I bet you do, but I DIDN'T. But I like to bite off challenges." Moments later, I was embarrassed to learn that this woman was the editor of a singles magazine! If I had been more mature, I might have been less intent, have been able to put my talk temporarily on hold, and perhaps have thought to say something like "How do you mean?" or "Why do you say that?"

Too many supervisors and managers are, without seeming to try, impetuous "tellers," intent on implementing their own ideas and solving problems their own way. (An advertising senior vice president of new markets once admitted at a meeting, "I found it difficult to listen without interrupting or giving my viewpoint. I missed some of the points because I was thinking about my responses.") An apt description of such hyperverbal folks might be "Blinded by his reflex to steamroll over any colleague who differed with him, he was effectively suppressing any ideas but his own." You have to know what your people—and customers—are thinking and concerned about to achieve consensus, and they must have a sense of trust before letting you know.

Typically, such talkers, armed with dedication and verbal fluency, possess scant technique in feeding back and collaborating with others in mutual relationship building. Lacking sufficient listening awareness, knowledge, and tools to bar distraction or respond creatively, they fail to capitalize on the *influence potential* of feedback to create a more congenial connection between themselves and others.

Why the Urge to Talk?

What makes us so eager to "free our ears from bondage" and make the other party listen to us? Why do we seem more thoroughly in our element when we are giving out rather than taking in?

In a newspaper account of a women's tennis championship match, one of the finalists was quoted as saying, "I just don't think I was calm. I wanted to hit the ball before it could even get over the net." (She lost that set.)

I recall, not proudly, in my early selling days calling on a particular prospect and telling him my story. I did most of the talking, asking few questions. I evidently overstayed my welcome because, after a while, I noticed his eyes had begun to glaze over. The meeting—and the sales opportunity—had abruptly ended.

We have largely bought into the conventional wisdom that persuades us that we are in the driver's seat when we are doing the talking. But this plays into a false stereotype of the listener as a weak, passive individual pitted against a much stronger, active figure. It's then no surprise that a lot of us, even unconsciously, preferably opt to be the speaker and give in to the seductive pull of self-indulgence.

That's why, in interactions with others, few have mastered the challenges of social coordination—listening with speaking, processing with participation—which are to be manipulated with considerable flexibility and in different directions for best results. We need to bring more subtlety and nuance to our highly charged drive to tell our story or remedy another's dilemma.

Getting More from Talking Less

Nothing impacts communication performance more than good balance. Successful listeners know when to be deferential. It has been suggested that "Without style, ambition is merely aggressive." This doesn't mean that self-interest is wrong, but that we need to apply the brakes sometimes and give another some airspace.

Engaging listeners hear more than their own words. They show quick response and notable resilience. They double back, interject to raise a query, and then concentrate anew in pursuit of full understanding. They then take away more value from conversations.

A CEO of a manufacturing company, whom I had coached, once told me: "The most difficult thing I have to do at work is suppress my ego and distraction long enough to let people say what they want to say, and for me to listen and get the content—whether a customer telling me what product(s) he wants to see developed, or an employee wanting to adjust machinery and work schedules. If I can listen long enough, they'll tell me what to do." He then added: "If I can hold back and keep away from what I *think* should be done, and just listen, I can double my business without any problem!"

How honest and true. We can't assess other people's "wants" unless we somehow temper our own. At times, the greatest distinguishing force can be self-restraint, but the hard part is in knowing how to build togetherness while maintaining autonomy. On the surface, conversation seems one way: the speaker gives, and the listener simply takes. But conversational currents need to flow in both directions if the parties are to realize optimal value from their time together. *And there can be more parity than we imagine.*

Ultimately, the effective listener is a receiver who also talks, not a talker who also receives. As we work to balance listening readiness against a certain need to be heard, greater self-awareness and listening know-how will help. We must realize that feedback and response keep the tendency to overtalk and dominate under tasteful restraint, making it easier to reassert self-control. This, in turn, will allow for smoother, and fairer, alternating of speaking turns. Interacting with a speaker's message through *restatement, acknowledgment,* and *questioning* will go far toward demonstrating the goodwill effort to understand and making the conversation mutually productive and satisfying.

Inputs and Outputs: Shuttling Between Two Poles

Allocating conversation time more evenhandedly between listening and speaking is one kind of balance. Another is coordinating mental work and social work.

Businesses today connect electronically via Internet, data, voice, and telephone systems, but how well do they connect *personally*? Whether in sales, employment interviews, team management, project and staff meetings, or telephone conversations, concentration alone is not enough to develop a speaker's trust. Partial listening dramatically reduces the quality of relationships, and poor relationships negatively impact morale and a company's balance sheet.

Conversation is a joint operation between listener and speaker. Both parties may be trying to work together, but not always operating in sync. Indeed, as the speaker's words move along, the listener may find him or herself in pursuit or getting ahead of the speaker. (Sometimes, for example, we listen to the first part of a conversation, then start to think how the information would impact us and how we'd handle it, and end up missing most of the content that follows.) This is the classic syndrome of listener with speaker: focus oftentimes goes to judgment, reaction, or rebuttal, and connection gets short shrift. The problem, of course, is how to bind two or more distinct minds to a single purpose and in the same time frame.

Balancing Two Opposing Values

We need to rethink the relationship between listeners and their speaking partners. Interestingly, when people talk about being between worlds, they usually mean cultural dislocation of a geopolitical sort. But listeners, too, are caught between worlds, two allegiances—different, yet complementary: their frame of reference and another's. We face the twin difficulties of not only taking in information but also giving out signals. Often inwardly divided, ours is the daunting task of having to judiciously navigate between these two poles. Effective conversation requires the listener to keep alternating between the roles of processor and participant, concentrator and collaborator. To get the biggest return on your investment of

time and effort, you have to go past the boundaries of your own temperament and judgment, at least for a time. Greater facility in managing these
complementary abilities can bring a different outcome. Paradoxically, the
more we involve ourselves in the conversation, the more focused, understandable, and memorable the message becomes. (In the words of one of
my workshop participants, "By asking questions I feel much more involved, get the message, and signal my interest and concern.")

Concentration can be, and often is, offset by weakness in cultivating
the relationship. Yet, by mastering the art and craft of existing in both
realms, we actually bridge the gap between ourselves and others. Such
listening provides a link to better interpersonal contact and a sounder
basis for building and expanding a management or sales relationship.

Some people just know how to listen. They seem to have a natural
ability to grasp what another is saying and an affinity for feedback. Many
of us, though, tend to take a speaker's words to be gratuitous, calling for
little reaction or response on our part. We have decided that the pursuit
of meaning comes first, with obligations to the speaker a distant runner-
up. (A cost analyst attending my workshop once confided that "Sometimes I become so intent on listening that I concentrate on listening rather
than actually listening.")

How freely do we give ourselves to others? For example, how often do
we let someone know his or her message is getting through? How readily
do we acknowledge the other person's feelings? ("The biggest issue is
probably that I intend to go right to the solution, failing to signal intent
and concern," confided a materials operation manager in my program.)
Do we check in with the speaker periodically to see whether we have
properly understood the message and to show that we are trying to
understand? (A recruiting manager in a training session once told me,
"I'm so eager to move on when I agree, I forget to let them know 'I got it'
or check 'Did I get it right?'")

Many of us have an overriding tendency to restrict our listening
essentially to intake. We are concerned, as we should be, about getting the
message straight. But much of the time, we are so preoccupied with analyzing our own reactions and studying our own attitudes that we may hear
much and see much, but absorb little. As listeners, we present quietly, stoic
and unmoving. Rarely do we share our mental life with our partners. We
appear to listen *on condition of anonymity*, as though anything we think or
feel is privileged information. (A candid software analyst explained, "Dealing with technical issues, I forget the human side.")

But there is an odd imbalance here, because feedback is a key element
of conversation, and every speaker knows it. When I was coauthoring an

article with a research psychiatrist, I came to one of our brainstorming meetings proudly excited to share some paragraphs and ideas I had put together. After a few moments of sharing, I felt a certain discomfort. Ignoring it, I went on relating my thoughts until it became clear that something was wrong. When I came to a grinding halt and looked up at my coauthor, he was smiling and said, "I just wanted to see how long you would go on without any feedback or response." I suddenly realized that he had deliberately withheld all signs of his listening—all the customary signals we unconsciously expect a listener to provide as markers along the road we *think* our message is taking—not to be insensitive, but to make this point: What we all crave is to be listened to *and to sense it.*

Mutual Benefits of Complete Listening

Feedback accomplishes many things. It lets the speaker know whether, and to what extent, the message has been received and understood; but it also brings the listener back into the conversation. It may reflect and validate the speaker's feelings, but it also helps us weather our own emotional storms. Feedback and response contribute to a lively pace and make conversation more efficient. Such gestures tilt the interpersonal playing field in the listener's favor (actually, in both parties' favor). The two sides are bent to the same intent, and there is more collegiality in the performance. (Recall the last time someone reacted with emotion to your personal plight or good news.) As listeners, we're only half functioning when feedback is not given a high priority. We coexist in the conversation, but don't combine. And this common failing in too many business engagements squanders the opportunity to get more out of a conversation by bringing two people closer.

Someone once observed, "Most people like to see reflections of themselves." When speakers hear their words through a listener's ears, or see themselves mirrored in the listener's face, they feel received, understood, even accepted. The two participants now function as true conversation partners, a duo. There is a sense of negotiation: *the easy understanding of when it is one's moment to be top dog and when it is not.* One might say that there is a new spirit of bipartisanship.

This is not always easy. Not all speakers have enough presence to hold our attention. But then, we don't always have enough presence to *reflect* it. As listeners, we owe speakers more than we give them on many occasions. One of the listener's unwritten mandates is to sometimes more fully acknowledge what the speaker is saying, to reflect back the speaker's mood. With this more direct contact between parties, there can be deeper understanding and closer relationships can develop.

Like a good historical writer successfully fusing the quaint with the contemporary, the best listeners are those who blend focus and feedback with an unwavering commitment to the speaker. They are not only keen observers but also adept *participants*: like cultural anthropologists, participant-observers. They have learned to think in two directions simultaneously, and you can too.

Observe others as they listen. Notice how, when data gathering and problem solving, people are very slow to make their entrance on the stage of conversation. There is a coy pulling back from response. We commonly see a silent, no-motions-wasted style of listening. Instead of thinking, as we should, "How can I let my partner know that I understand what she is saying and sense how she feels?", we end up thinking, "Who really cares?" or "When do I get a word in here?" Commuting uneasily between the poles of focus and feedback, we overlook genuine opportunities to show respect and empathy, to forge a congenial connection that would yield more value for all concerned. And so we typically hide our thoughts and feelings behind a mask of sober detachment.

A participant in my speaking workshop once told me, "It all comes down to one thing: getting past yourself." I pondered those words for some time. A recent experience I had cast some light on this.

Driving along one day, I noticed a car parked in front of me alongside the curb. It suddenly started up and veered into my lane. The driver went a short distance and, again without warning, abruptly turned right at the next corner. No signal of intent, no thought of anyone else on the road besides himself. Locked inside his own head, he was unable to get past himself.

In conversation, we tend to do much the same thing. Why are we frugal with our feedback? What makes us so reluctant to respond?

CHAPTER 2

The Listening Leader—A First Approximation

Reception and understanding have traditionally been the lens for listening. Now, much more so, collaboration is. In today's business world, the true leader is expected to take responsibility not only for his or her understanding but also for *being understanding*.

The Distorting Lens of Tradition

In much modern listening practice, traditional notions of stylistic propriety hold sway. Few of us, as we have seen, realize how much of the time we tend to withhold feedback in conversations with others. With scant response and few comments or rejoinders, the style is basically introspective. (Like investors shunning global risk, we prefer to stay close to home.)

A friend of mine once told me a story of his taking some clothes to the laundry. As he handed them to the woman at the counter, he made some request. When there was no response from her, he repeated himself as politely as he could. The response then was "OK. I HEAR you!" (annoyance instead of acknowledgment).

Now consider this piece of overheard conversation: A man, complaining about his landlord, said: "... and then he takes six months away from us—there's no FAIRNESS with this guy!" A disinterested bystander replies: "Yeah" (little involvement, generic response).

A Limiting Legacy

For long stretches in conversation we seem to be just keeping an eye on things. This listening-at-arm's-length attentiveness—what I call *listener protocol*—is more than social indiscretion. We noted earlier that it comes with a high price tag—whether in sales, one-to-one conversations, meetings, or interviews. It leaves the speaker a bit abandoned. A starched listening style robs the conversation of its life pulse, restricting information flow and increasing the level of stress and dissatisfaction. And this widespread tendency is deeply imprinted in all of us.

Imagine in your own performance appraisal, or some other meeting with your supervisor, explaining yourself and getting no sign of life. Did he hear you? Does he understand? Is he fully present? *Does he care?* What's worse, your very success—as a manager, team leader, salesperson, friend—is imperiled by a bland demeanor that has become the norm in most conversations.

A Refreshing Change

To be sure, we are not always so deficient. I had a most unusual conversation during a taxi ride in Massachusetts. While the driver was taking me to Logan Airport to catch a flight back home, we began talking about listening. As the discussion developed, we both found ourselves willing and interested partners—being drawn more and more into a deeply shared focus. The effortless flow of conversation, and the strong sense of mutuality, made for an exhilarating and enjoyably short trip. There seemed not to be a single moment when our concentration slipped. Forty-five minutes later, when he dropped me off, we said good-bye and thanked each other for a most interesting and pleasurable experience—both of us professing to having been *fully present for the entire trip*.

Admittedly, this is extremely rare. But we can infuse some of the successful elements of such an experience into many interactions, getting much more out of them. In succeeding chapters we will find out how.

A Compartmentalized Identity and Role

For now, let's look at this point: Like the moon, we are sometimes vividly present; at other times, we seem to be hidden or offstage. Why is this so?

Unconscious, tradition-bound attitudes severely distort the ways we understand, manage, and derive benefit from listening.

As some point out, "It's hard to grow up in America and not buy into some of the communication mythology and have that go to work in your conversations." Talk is often perceived by a listener as a self-standing event, sustained by tacit understanding.

So we unconsciously subscribe to the belief that to listen is, essentially, to be an *absorbing head*. (We can't get away with this in speaking, because a talking head hardly claims listener allegiance!) Convention consigns listening to an intellectual exercise and reduces the listener to a cerebral cortex.

We have thoughts, feelings, and impulses, but seem unable to act on them. Listener responsiveness shuts down despite our better instincts because, in part, we operate under a set of unwritten rules that discourages expressiveness and encourages retreat from the speaker. It does not present itself; we apprehend it. Deadpan and frozen in place, our reticence seems motivated more by conformance to a received standard of behavior than by deliberate design. And we carry out our prescribed roles not so much because we derive pleasure from it but because we don't know how to escape.

Self-Image

It may also be that we come to our role from a sense of being on the margins of social interaction—the presumption that the listener is a bit player in the game of conversation. We thus see ourselves cast in a minor, supporting role, much like, in a piano recital, a page-turner, one of those discreet, anonymous figures who stand at the pianist's side, flipping pages as the music unscrolls in the concert hall. So fixed is that norm in our unconscious mind that many of us have difficulty breaking through the constrictions and limits defined by it. (At new-product development meetings, an associate product manager has found it "... often difficult to communicate that I am listening. I am often asked, 'Are you following me?' or 'Is this getting through to you?'") For listeners, then, coming to terms with these realities means more than skills training. It means confronting our own social/interpersonal legacies.

Also, listeners face unnecessary pressure in withholding response, not unlike concert soloists who feel compelled by convention to perform a musical piece completely from memory. The protocol is deeply entrenched.

Observe the typical business conversation and watch how people interact. Ironically, despite the eye contact and seeming concentration, they are not more absorbed in the message; *they are more removed from it.* It is a disturbingly negative and lonely experience.

Listeners find nonresponding onerous, yet cannot buck the protocol dictating that listening behavior be limited essentially to attending. For listeners who have difficulty with responding—not knowing what to say, or when to interject—the pressure can be unsettling. (In one of my workshops, an administrative assistant sought to be able to feel more confident about what kind of questions she should ask to better understand the speaker.) We seem to be carefully trying never to cover the speaker's voice. Sometimes, this deference can be by choice, but the conversational balance is off.

Contrary to the received wisdom, attentiveness—shorn of familiar elements such as verbal response, questions, and facial expression—is considerably disorienting to the average speaker. *This reserve also makes us secretive, quick to dissemble, and quicker to judge.* (According to a retail toy store assistant director in my workshop, "I think I miss opportunities to offer praise or encouragement to my associates because I categorize their concerns as whining.")

So why does the protocol persist? Basically the brain is a creature of habit. And it is reinforced by educators who still teach by the lecture method, generations of television watching, growing numbers of computer-screen addicts, and one's equally convention-bound friends and colleagues. They all falsely assume that a listener not silently paying attention is a rude listener.

Challenging the Conventional Wisdom

In one way or another, we have let our partners and ourselves down, but with little hope of significant change, we have gotten used to this situation. I wonder how many of us, in our heart of hearts, really like it this way. Yet, we put up with it anyway because that's the way it is. But that's not the way it has to be or should be. We need to consciously counteract this tendency in order to get the most from conversations and accomplish interpersonal goals. We must come to see feedback as a 'shaper' of conversation. If not, we may find accommodation and resignation, but rarely true rapport.

When we discipline ourselves to be as intent on enriching others as enriching ourselves, we can be more successful. Listeners are at their best and most memorable in showing themselves to be attentive *collaborators*, active discussants in the conversation, which provides more benefit for all.

Focus and Feedback: A Better Balance

On the surface, conversations are one way: the speaker gives, and the listener takes. Daily experience seems to bear this out, primarily because processing has long been a much higher priority for listeners than has participating. This fundamental dynamic has to change in its proportions before there can be progress in strengthening the listener's presence of mind and unlocking listening's leadership potential.

Listening remains a very difficult role to do well because listeners must be focused enough to concentrate, but forthcoming enough to collaborate. It is axiomatic that listeners in conversation need concentration power strong enough to keep distraction at bay. But equally crucial, if less fully appreciated, is a reactivity and responsiveness vivid enough to create contact and maintain connection.

We have seen that listeners have become outsiders of sorts, marginalized by history. They tend to lead highly circumscribed existences, doing what they see other listeners do. When we listen to someone speak, we overly focus on intake. We hold ourselves apart from the speaker, which makes full tracking difficult. Today, too many listeners are passively sitting by, forfeiting feedback and commitment to the speaker in favor of focus and self-interest. True to form, we contain ourselves, hardly releasing a smile. We may permit ourselves a degree of head nodding and grunting (humming sounds) but draw the line at response. Nothing is more common than salespeople and managers who pursue goals that cannot be fulfilled because of inherent flaws in such one-sided listening styles. Speakers, after a while, miss a listener's truancy. There is a strange disparity between inbound and outbound listening, which engenders conversation that has more to do with separation than with contact. And it contributes to making our time in conversation a period of lost opportunities.

A Responsive Presence

Yet in the most basic way, listeners are defined not by the messages they receive or their politics or their gender or their race, *but by the responses they make*. We must understand what we are being told, but couple that with acknowledgment, response, and a fuller sense of involvement. Whether you are in management or sales, it is important to affect people the way you need to. We tend to forget that subordinates, coworkers, and customers must *sense* that you take them and their concerns seriously. This means creating a true dialogue in which both parties feel free to share and receive relevant information.

Leaders know how to react. The responsive moment is valued almost as much as it is in replying to a question. And they will make an appropriate comment without being prompted. To paraphrase no less a leader than Franklin D. Roosevelt, *better the occasional misunderstandings of a listener who lives in a spirit of charity than the consistent omissions of a listener frozen in the ice of his own indifference.*

Feedback

To help professionals expand their listening-response repertoire (what a friend and neighbor recently called a "response arsenal"), we introduce in our programs the concept of *key phrases*. This is a list of things you might say in response to what someone is telling you. Choosing from more options generates greater freedom of expression.

What will emerge from this will be more easily achieving connection and contact, and eliciting more consistent and helpful messages. For example, to a coworker who may be sharing with you her frustration over a thorny issue she is facing, you might say: "It's hard to put up with that when you don't have any control over it." Perhaps in another situation in which a colleague describes his difficult, but successful, transition into a new department and position in the company, you might say: "It sounds like it worked out for you." Or after presenting your point of view on a subject, and your boss or colleague says, "I agree with you, more or less," you might inquire (with a slight grin), "Why less?"

For many listeners, though, the journey of staying focused and seeking understanding in conversation is a lonely, solitary struggle. Our listening seems to be zipping along. We may seem to have matters pretty well in hand, but then we suddenly hit a dry patch. Our mind slips into another realm altogether. Too much burden on focus alone cannot be sustained. We quickly use up our ration of concentration unless we reach out and make contact with another. It is worth remembering that when responding recedes into the background, much of the conversation's energy is lost, abandoning the speaker to navigating uncharted waters without a compass. What follows is *conversation at a distance.*

Some old habits in listening die hard. The two phases of listening—taking in and giving out—can go hand in hand but require nimble coordination. The listener must change hats. Even accomplished listeners are not immune to the tension exerted by this challenge of moving between autonomy and interdependence, between internal and external listening. I have often thought that this dual aspect of listening bears resemblance to a pianist-conductor who alternates between playing the piano and leading the orchestra during the performance of a piano concerto. Few would argue that this is easy. But with practice, as we will see in a later chapter, you can learn to dispatch responses with an air of spontaneity, giving the impression that your words are being thought up on the spot.

Accomplished listeners recognize that feedback is the social currency that private rumination is not. Feedback puts the brakes on distraction, revs listeners up mentally, and allows them to regain a sense of focus and self-control. In any listening relationship, they realize that speakers have trouble reading the varieties of intent behind "mmm's" and so make their responses more precise. With feedback, we may even discover a much more interesting and diverse personality across the way from us. In turn, we become a more approachable presence. Clarifying and affirming re-affirm our commitment to the conversation.

Interruption or Intervention?

Knowing how to respond is one thing. Knowing *when* to intervene, or interject, is quite another. We may consider responding, but often it remains unrealized—perpetually pending—something like an overdue report that isn't out yet. We assume that almost any comment or question we offer up is an unwarranted infringement on the speaker's right to self-expression or, worse yet, is taking reckless liberties. And so we fret over its perception as an interruption, worrying that it may be a breach of polite conduct. Our ambivalence may extend even to the point of not overtly reacting in a normally expected manner. Listening then becomes an exercise in thwarted response.

Listeners have a right—if not an obligation—to let a speaker know how much of the message they have received and with what effect on them. You could argue that this is overstepping bounds. Although that may seem true, listeners might have something relevant to contribute, or they might need to move the speaker or group along because of time constraints. So how can listeners deal more effectively with this almost moral quandary?

One of the services a speaker can do for his or her listeners is to offer occasional silence, a pause, to get a word in. Unfortunately most speakers get on a roll and find self-restraint beyond them.

Getting a Word in Edgewise

Some help comes, though, from another source: the research literature on turn-taking signals (see, for example, Duncan, 1975). Studies show, for example, that when one wishes to say something in conversation or at a meeting, one can signal this intent by

- slightly changing body positioning,
- using some slight hand gesture, and then
- *italicizing* his or her spoken words.

The combination of these behaviors has the effect of getting the speaker's attention—and communicating the listener's desire to add something to the discussion. This may not work with every speaker (or meeting leader), but it will generally shift the percentages in the direction of success (so you don't have to be a human "pressure cooker"). You might try it. Remember that intervening—not interrupting—requires as much courage as tact. Here, again, practice will allow you to make a smoother transition into the conversational arena more often.

A New Flexibility

Among the critical lessons to be drawn from all this is the need for a new listening flexibility: the idea that focus and feedback should not be limited by one's personal agenda or bias. Just as in speaking, there is a difference between what listeners intend to communicate and what they actually communicate. Greater success is realized in a comprehensive strategy that emphasizes collaboration as well as concentration. This is listening that is *fully realized*.

We have the freedom to take a different road, to chart a new course in our listening life. We can make the listening process work more successfully by changing the intake-to-response ratio. This new balance will demolish the quarantine between the speaker and listener by increasing the interplay among all parties, and enable one to muster a more tightly intertwined dialogue that will foster and nurture relationships.

From Understanding to Influence

Once we have understood the message, we have been conditioned to think that our job as listener is over. Which is why many of us approach listening as a solo activity, conceiving of it as an independent art, a process that goes on only in our mind. (Notice that the traditional thinking is not only a convention for keeping thoughts and feelings inside the head but also a way of preventing a kind of holistic view of conversation. It is feedback that allows us to think of conversation *as a single space*.) Tightly tethered to that little voice in our head, and protective of our privacy, our listening is not usually a matter of public record. So we tend to be low-profile listeners, and watching the way most others play the listener role in conversation only reinforces this accustomed notion of listening.

In some ways, listeners have become prisoners of traditional norms and the straitjacketed style they impose. They feel trapped and closed in by the narrow terms. The overly buttoned-up manner and its tendency to inhibit natural expression, pulse, and rhythm must lead one to question a style that makes it virtually impossible to show interest and truly engage another.

Why, for example, do so many wives and workers complain that husbands and bosses don't listen? Not infrequently, women in my seminars say to me, "My husband should take your course." Others chime in with "Top management should be here." Are spouses and supervisors really not listening or only *partially* listening?

Notice how often people leave a conversation or meeting feeling dissatisfied and unfulfilled. There must be more to it. And there is. *We need to breach the border to connection.*

Listening As Influence

At the outset, I used the term *influential* to describe a certain type of listening. This word may have struck some readers as strangely inappropriate in front of the word *listening*. But managers can, to some degree, be the architects of their own situations *even when playing the listener role.*

Paraphrasing the recent words of a physician whose letter had appeared in the Science Times section of the New York Times, a leader's ability to listen has great symbolic value to others in the organization. This skill goes to the core of what it is to be a leader—the exercising of influence. Even in this time of technology, management seems to cherish that. Independent of communication value and cost effectiveness is the value of establishing that connection. It contributes to the associate's comfort and satisfaction, and it may even have motivational value.

This doctor has well captured the essence of listening's two dimensions: concentration and collaboration. Focus is one thing; feedback is another. And processing is one thing, and participation is another. We need to broaden the definition of listening to encompass response and feedback— to disabuse ourselves of the notion that full-fledged listening consists *only* of absorbing and understanding what we hear. What makes conversations work is the listener's consistent powers as an insightful commentator on the speaker's text, an attentive collaborator. It's hard to discount the importance of feedback in conversation, but somehow we manage. And so most supervisors don't have enough presence to be influential.

Failure to disclose our registering the message is all too common (as we have observed). When we don't respond, it may be because we are thinking or perhaps being considerate. But is this always so? Feeding back to a speaker translates into higher engagement and improves the compatibility between conversational partners. The dialogue becomes more porous, more open to genuinely expressed feelings and deeper understanding. Speaker and listener become more at ease with one another. By holding back, we may sow seeds of uncertainty as our "secret life" makes us an unknown and unknowable entity.

Our detachment even extends often to not acknowledging the speaker's emotional overtones. Attentive but disengaged with stoic demeanor, the average manager does not cut the figure of a commanding leader. And with silence, immobility, and expressive restraint, he or she seems more a cardboard figure than a dynamic partner.

The yardstick by which business measures listening success is often the experienced employee who provides a ready answer to another's problem or need. But even here, a more engaging listening style makes the speaker more ready to appreciate, and accept, the solution.

Reaching Out to Speakers

Wider success in listening—and the ability to motivate others—calls for different rules of conduct, a style more consistently balanced in its mix of processing and responding. In this sense, listening is no less real or primary than speech. It is a form of *literacy*, what we could call performance literacy. It is a tribute to the supervisor's self-management and stewardship of the conversation that others can feel safe enough to communicate more openly.

I once visited a friend whose father had just passed away. She, the youngest daughter, related how her father as a young man had come from Europe to the United States and taken a post teaching after school hours. She described how students and faculty perceived his being so vibrant and exuberant. At one point, I ventured, "He really pumped new life into the school." Her eyes lit up. She responded to me with noticeably heightened focus, alertness, and expression: on her face, in her voice, and in her overall demeanor. She seemed more alive, grateful to hear her words picked up and appreciated.

Through flexible responding, managers can create a motivational environment in which associates will be more focused, forthcoming, and honest. Indeed, power is there for the taking.

But we are too often a spectator at our own events, only grudgingly yielding up some minimal sign of acknowledgment. As listeners, we often feel powerless and voiceless in the conversational arena. In holding back, we seem to give ourselves room to expand and indulge our thoughts and feelings with a certain freedom and distance. But without connection, our thoughts will eventually stray. It is in responding that the listener becomes an expansive and memorable figure. *As listeners, we don't find our identity until we find our voice.*

The Power of an Affecting Presence

To overcome a sense of separation, we need to come in from the bleachers once in a while and get into the game, to move from onlooker to player, *to break out of the mold and make contact.* In this way, we can have a more positive effect on our conversational partners, the relationship, and ourselves. How much more effective we are when we more fully disclose our listening!

The manager's trademark reserve—her minimalist impulse—is ill-suited to today's team-based environment, relationship selling, and effectively functioning groups. When we don't give much hint of the private activity going on inside our heads, the speaker has no real sense of our getting the message—no real understanding, for that matter, of his or her own status. *To be connected is to feel worth.* Reclusiveness robs the speaker of self-realization. So don't keep all your thinking in your head—express it.

Listeners owe their partners, and themselves, a listening style that gives thought and response equal billing. A passive listening to the speaker, anything less than a full involvement with the message, will give only an inadequate notion of the meaning, let alone the way the listener feels about it. Moreover, the message can be lost to us amid a commotion of competing thoughts and feelings. But more frequently, creative responding can, in fact, be an act of influence. Here follows a striking example.

I remember flying to California to provide listening training to a senior team of customer service executives at a large high-tech corporation. I had been told that the impetus for this was an important meeting they were to have the following week in Florida with some of their major direct customers.

We spent an enjoyable, productive day together. In the afternoon, something striking happened. As two participants were about to be videotaped (again) while holding a conversation, one partner turned to the group and said, "We hold opposite views of how our company should conduct business." That comment immediately grabbed everyone's attention.

As we watched, we were all privy to some of the most open, nondefensive, mutually affirming communication I have ever seen. When the brief conversation ended, it was clear to everyone that, although the parties did not resolve their differences, they would gladly have agreed to discuss more.

Upon observing the playback, all of us were struck by two more revelations: Each side had effectively clarified the other's thinking, and, even beyond that, each one had made of the other a more articulate speaker. (Now, if that's not *influence*, I have to go back and look up the word in the dictionary again!)

This rewarding conversation, although rare, shows what can happen when an insightful and trust-inspiring listener partners with an adept speaker who is as much steeped in the collaborative practice of reciprocity. The results are clearheaded intelligence and productive dialogue. So direct was the contact between listener and speaker that they made surprisingly good partners. Both sides possessed the verbal and mental capacity—and commitment—to regard the other as an equal. Each, by turns, gave the other the *assurance of undivided attention and voiced respect.*

Pushing the traditional envelope beyond focus and concentration also serves another purpose: it interrupts our personal time scheme to contribute some reaction or response. This can be a welcome relief from the constant pressure of having to process input. We can then resume our intake with renewed interest and focus.

Responsiveness may be the road less traveled, but it leads to better results. You don't succeed in conversation just by showing up. Like the lottery, "you have to be in it to win it." And like a stock return, you receive a gain and a dividend.

Leadership listening is *organized and demonstrative* listening. The more willing managers are to make its presence manifest—to color outside the lines—the more forthcoming associates tend to be. Better put, small and frequent doses of responding have a disproportionately large impact on a speaker. Instead of consuming valuable time engaging in cagey conversation, they tend to open up the books and let their true thoughts and feelings be known. Real issues are revealed. Common ground is discovered and plowed together. Bonds are strengthened and time is optimized.

CHAPTER 3

Attitudes and Demons

Listeners in the last century did not see feedback as having a significant bearing on the conduct of their listening. So they were especially victimized by the negative effects of other factors—a filled and set mind, the conviction that speakers have the primary obligation to draw listeners' attention, distraction, distortion, and defensiveness—on their listening. This set of attitudes and listening demons will be covered in this chapter.

The Filled Mind

Are you really ready to listen? When you get on the phone or begin a face-to-face conversation, are you mentally prepared to fully focus on the here-and-now and give the other person your undivided attention?

Much talk has a hard time making its way into an already crowded mind (have you ever tried squeezing just one more article into a full suitcase?). In listening, as in life, one can be overprogrammed. Even before a conversation begins, most of us are on overload. The many things buzzing around in our head—the intellectual stuff, the emotional baggage that's too much with us—vie for our attention. Our spirit sags under the weight of this mental clutter. And quantity of information puts pressure on quality of performance.

Realistically, we need to make the conversation a priority in order to raise our expectation of achieving something of value for ourselves and others. We must try to free up our minds—by a conscious act of will—to discover some reward for spending time with another's message.

Daily Intrusions

Kyle, a line manager at a major computer chip manufacturer, was just about to finally crack that recommended management leadership book that had been gathering dust on his desk when the phone rang. His boss's secretary was letting him know of a division line managers meeting that had just been called to discuss a very important matter. It was being held in Conference Room B, and Kyle was expected to attend. As he reluctantly put down the unopened book, he was upset by this sudden, unwelcome interruption. "Another waste of time," he thought. Walking out into the hall, he wondered, "Why now? What 'very important matter'?"

He arrived in the meeting room to find several of his colleagues already there, all buzzing with anticipation and expectations of what the issue at hand might be. Kyle walked over to where John, a line manager with many more years at the company than he, was standing. "Hey, what's going on?" Kyle asked. "I really don't go for these 'all-important meetings'—most of them are just an exercise in futility, a lot of people talking past each other. I've got better things to do with my time." John smiled knowingly and said: "You mean you were just in the middle of something and, besides, nobody listens anyway?" "Yeah, exactly," Kyle agreed. "I know how you feel, buddy," said John affably, "but the way I look at it, if I can take away one thing of value from a meeting, that's worth something." "You're saying to go in with a positive attitude ...." "I'd say so," confirmed John. "It usually works better that way." Kyle wasn't fully convinced, but he respected John's judgment and was willing to give it a try.

The ability to control the contents of our mind is ours, but we must be willing to exercise it. Adopting a positive attitude—and the tools to maintain it—will help keep us in a more receptive frame of mind.

But the events we carry around in our heads—leftovers from previous discussions, fragmented bits of anticipated experience, personal concerns—often come along with us to our meetings and contacts. Such things already residing in our minds inhabit our attention and crowd out potential newcomers. What is said then becomes dynamically hazy because the words are heard as through a mist. These days, it does indeed take greater effort to focus and more willpower to get a grip on our concentration. How can we dislodge what's in our heads? What does it take to wipe the mental slate clean? Must a listener's mind be empty to be open? Ad hoc seems the order of the day. The average listener's mode of operation is to muddle through as best he or she can, hoping that the speaker or subject or both will bail him or her out. But better answers to these questions must be found if we are to ease the listener's plight and avoid some serious dislocations in conversations and meetings.

Breaking through Mental Clutter

Recognize that the issue here is one not only of crowding but also of attitude and personal responsibility. To be sure, there is too much commotion in the minds of today's listeners, which is one of many factors working against us. Keeping so much information upstairs causes stress, and if we don't somehow release some of the pent-up pressure in our heads and hearts, distraction takes over. We are then expressively inert— a condition that comes at the expense of fostering an environment that allows for full, open communication.

No matter what kind of talking encounter we are engaged in, we tend to sit shrouded in the cramped cocoon of private thinking. Feeling and being cut off from another impoverishes understanding. The brain may be churning; but much of what the speaker is saying, and how she feels about it, goes largely unnoticed and unacknowledged. Because this condition severely cuts down on our receptivity, we have to work harder to pay attention. The extreme time pressure to meet deadlines, the weight of having to meet quotas, and other daily concerns constitute a formidable distraction from the present moment. This obviously reduces the chance of the conversation or meeting becoming a high-gain transaction for speaker and listener alike. The central question is: What can be done— what are we willing to do—to cope with this situation?

Connecting with others—either mentally in an audience or with overt expression in a conversation—can ease the listener's psyche. It redirects our energies away from competing concerns, to concentrate more fully on the speaker and message at hand instead. In addition to feeling refocused, we increase the chances of gaining much greater benefit from the time everyone is spending.

The Set Mind

Whereas crowded minds resist penetration, judgments—too quick and subjective—further constrict listening: We often seem to have made up our minds ahead of time. Most people let their listening revolve around personal likes and dislikes. Many have a cafeteria-approach to listening: "I will listen if I agree, and if I don't, I won't."

People tend to have strong opinions. Proverbial is our penchant for seeing the world in moralistic categories of black and white, good or evil, right or wrong. Some people seem to carry a mental courtroom around with them wherever they go, believing in judgment at first sight (or hearing). Can there ever really be an objective esthetic? Cultural and individual factors may suggest not.

We pride ourselves on being acutely perceptive. But perceptions can play tricks. Often, people are more complex than the pigeonholes we place them in might suggest. What's more, much of our understanding has been scripted in advance. Earlier experiences in a sense dictate our perceptions (somewhat akin to program notes to a concert piece). We filter facts through the strainer of past knowledge and experience, which can skew our reading of individuals and messages. We remain blissfully unaware of how much this prior knowledge narrows our breadth of thought and perspective. *Every new thing that enters our heads collides with what is already there.*

The Rush to Judgment

Judgment is a force that can sometimes grip the listener's mind from the get-go and refuse to relinquish its hold. In conversational terms, others are not best captured in a snapshot, but in a moving picture or videotape. Like some photographs, some people may seem utterly unprepossessing (small impressions can take on major significance), yet close attention to them can be rewarding. Delaying judgment provides fresh listening experiences. Only by deferring judgment can new information enter a more yielding mind, providing the listener with a fuller, more nuanced understanding. For example, a colleague expresses to you his personal feelings or concerns on a matter, and you unthinkingly respond, "Oh, you shouldn't feel that way," or "I wouldn't let that bother me." You may not have intended it, but this judgmental reaction effectively denies your coworker's legitimate feelings. He may suddenly regret having revealed his personal side. But an empathetic response—such as "And you find that upsetting," or "I can see how that could be frustrating"—goes far toward erasing any misgivings the speaker may harbor.

We judge others and their subject through many inputs: look, sound, and words. Appearance does much to guide our perceptions: the speaker's height and build, dress and demeanor. We make a judgment based on what we see. But the ear may yet be applied with qualities the eye might have been denied. One's delivery may be slow, plodding, and lethargic. The content may put us off; in our inner ear something says, "That doesn't make sense!" Or the speaker may express ideas that clash with our own. More generally, the overriding tendency is to see things only from our own viewpoint and vantage point (interestingly, a camera cannot refuse to see what it sees the way humans can).

Extremists cannot acknowledge any competing value nor give weight to another point of view. We seize upon aspects of divergence (what Freud called "the narcissism of small differences" in *The Psychopathology of Everyday Life*, 1901). This narrow-minded approach closes us off from experimentation and discovery. To appreciate a speaker's message, we need to take a balanced look at others. And, yes, we sometimes have to get past the speaking style.

When you rid yourself of overconcern for differences and listen for content, personal meaning, and nuance, you may find the message—and the person—more interesting than you first imagined.

Our interest in subjects or other people is too often one of comparison, not of pure curiosity about new information or the unique personality of another (some have the attitude of whatever isn't of interest or relevance to me isn't worth bothering with). We don't always want to hear what we don't already know. Or, we may assume that we're going to hear what we've already heard before. It's worth reminding ourselves to try not to tar every speaker with the same brush; otherwise, this "noise" can hang over our heads and close our minds to listening.

Attitude over Mind

Note that the tendency toward bias has more to do with the receivers than with what is being received. Try to make each experience before you as new as possible, similar to listening to yet another version of a familiar song or musical piece (this is not always easy). Savvy listeners listen respectfully, displaying an agreeably tolerant open-mindedness. This does not mean lack of discernment; rather, they don't close their minds on it too quickly. They remain inquisitive.

Yet, some critical intelligence needs to be at work. We don't have time to waste in "buying" every idea and person. But our evaluative temperament is a bit like nuclear fission: harnessed in the right way, it is a powerful tool for understanding, learning, and growing. And while we should not do away with judgment, we are sometimes better served by putting it on hold for a little while. If we can remember how we feel in the moment of being judged, that is a good beginning.

It's-the-Speaker's-Responsibility Attitude

That's not all that severely tests a listener's goodwill. Life is full of distractions. But poor, if well-intentioned, speakers compound the problem. "I am perfectly willing to listen as long as he makes it worth my while," said one general manager of an electrical utility in a seminar. "After all," she continued, "it's the one talking whose job it is to provide the interest, focus and motivation for me to pay attention. But how do speakers expect us to stay with them if they don't do their job right? They just don't seem to realize—most of them—that they need to cater to *our* needs." This attitude is quite common. To be sure, speakers have some *but not all* responsibility for listener success.

What Speakers Owe Listeners

Let's admit it. Speakers need to remember that most listeners operate on the principle of *least effort*: we are lazy and prefer a message carefully boxed and FedExed from the speaker's mouth to our ears. Because the typical speaker is not concerned about our needs, he or she falls short of our expectations. The ear, too often, has to fight through the verbal smog to get at the message's meaning. The narrative might be so densely packed with information that it would take at least two hearings for every detail to register.

We often chafe at the speaker's style of delivery. Frankly, it is difficult to care too much when:

- talk is too technical (easy-to-follow layman's language is not used);
- the voice is underprojected (the contribution does not register strongly);
- the rate is too fast (finding danger in lingering, many a speaker will not pause, allowing phrases to breathe, but seem bent on getting on with it);
- or the rate is too slow (lifeless, unflowing tempo).

Speakers wear out their welcome in other ways as well. Many, for example, unwittingly end up talking to themselves, as it were, by making communication one sided. Inwardly focused—and failing to include us in their remarks—they tend to be self-centered, self-serving, and ultimately self-defeating. I learned this the hard way when faced with my first experience in front of a training group. Finding others' suggestions to overcome nervousness completely unhelpful, I gave myself an intensive crash course in observing what other speakers do. I then discovered that most speakers unconsciously focus on themselves—in thoughts, words, and actions—and thereby fail to *engage* their audience in a more satisfying and successful joint venture. A speaker's self-focus, loose content, and weak delivery can stretch a listener's tenacity to excruciating lengths.

Some speakers will abruptly change subject or focus with no questions asked. This, too, is a form of noise that interferes with listeners getting the full message.

Brevity is the better part of valor, but not every speaker seems to know this. With today's rapid pace of living, many of us have a near zero tolerance for ideas that ripen slowly. We want the speaker to get unequivocally to the point; so when the message zigzags and lacks direction and stated purpose, we again suffer "ear trauma." And our several attempts to keep focused seem to stall out.

Words will make the message clear and meaningful when they speak to the eye as well as the ear; for example, through analogy, gestures, and word imagery. But few speakers take this into account.

As listeners, we have certain hopes and expectations that we fairly feel a speaker should meet: engage my attention, move and excite me, and I will pay attention. Speak boringly, incoherently, aimlessly, or talk about something I have no interest in, and you will lose me. (Listeners can be wrong about a subject's value, but they know what they like.)

What Listeners Owe Speakers

That said, however, we need to keep a proper perspective if we're going to salvage more value from listening. Let's admit that many of these "injuries" are self-inflicted or at least become ways of excusing failure. The weaker listeners among us tend to rely too insistently on the speaker doing all the work. Whether it is fair or not, speakers present themselves and their messages in the only way they know how at the time. To appreciate what is said, we sometimes need to overlook the manner of speaking, if possible, and dig into the message. (I still personally struggle to an extent with getting past a speaker's arrogant style.) It's a harsh fact of life, but not every speaker is clear, succinct, and engaging (most presentations, in fact, are astonishingly pedestrian).

I have found it to be a more realistic and *proactive* approach to say: "If I hold myself responsible for focusing and externalize my listening, I know I can be fully present." To truly understand this is to become a more accepting, and more responsive, communicator.

Granted, it means some more work, and our time is limited. But the effort to stay tuned—the willingness to take partial responsibility for success—can sometimes find its own reward: in putting others at their ease, capturing needed information, discovering new knowledge or insight, or simply—and importantly—*practicing our listening*. The speaker may not be up to carrying the full load him or herself and really should not have to. By pitching in and offering some help in support of the communication task, listeners not only display a generosity of spirit but also get better results.

The Listening Demons

Other things that bedevil the would-be listener are the listening demons: *distraction*, *distortion*, and *defensiveness*. These are often some of the hurdles that leadership stumbles over. How well we deal with our demons determines our success. Let's examine each one to see how we can keep them from getting the best of us.

Distraction

In our fast-moving, technology-driven world, distraction can invade every aspect of our lives and can even cause bodily harm. According to the American Automobile Association, "The National Transportation Safety Board recently estimated that up to 20% of all car accidents are caused by driver distractions such as mobile phones (on average 8,000 car accidents daily)." Several localities have now begun to enact legislation that will prohibit or reduce handheld cell phone use while driving.

Distraction knows no socioeconomic backgrounds, no geographic limitations. People of different shapes, sizes, and ethnic affiliations are all prone to its mind-robbing force.

It was an agonizingly long phone conversation that left you feeling emotionally drained and frustrated by its lack of resolution. Returning the phone to its cradle, you're suddenly aware of the pounding in your head and the tightness in your chest. Just then, one of your managers comes in to see you about a problem he's having with one of his people.

You struggle to concentrate on what he's telling you, but your efforts to keep focused fail as your mind continues to replay bits of that phone conversation. In the wake of these unsettling events, you try to rejoin the conversation that is already in progress, but find that you have missed too much to get back in sync. Whether due to outside sources, emotional stress, mental clutter, or fatigue, distraction is a fact of listening life. We all experience minor disconnects when our minds stray to other concerns, or associations are born during the conversational experience. At other times, we "change the channel" (click on a more stimulating icon). Our minds race ahead on fast-forward or retreat in rapid rewind. Either way, we sometimes seem to be in separate time zones and find ourselves out of step with the speaker or the present situation.

I was on line in my local post office one day when a woman in back of me asked, "Are you on line?" (Feeling a twinge of annoyance, my first impulse was to say, "Of course I'm on line!" but I found the grace not to blurt that out.) Looking around me, I realized that the line had moved up while I was momentarily lost in my thoughts. I then responded, "Yes, I am. Sorry."

Distraction is misdirected energy that siphons off our concentration. It is borrowing stimulation from another time or place for immediate consumption. Often distraction is not the thinking we will ourselves to do but the sort that comes along unbidden, sometimes in a trickle, sometimes in a flood.

Distraction may be imported or of the home-grown variety. Machines running, blowers blowing, competing conversations nearby, the constant interruptions and demands on our time—these are all outside our heads. We have little or no control over them. But what about the interference of our own making: the predispositions we bring to conversations, the judgments we make so quickly of others, or those land mines that can bump us off-line and take us out of our game?

Sometimes, we simply get snagged on an idea or something the speaker says, causing our mind to take an unplanned detour. I was talking with a client one day when his unexpected smile broke my momentum. Noticing the look of puzzlement on my face, he offered as explanation, "I was just out in Iowa. I have a good customer out there."

A more frequent trigger of distraction is *emotional reaction*. Many of us are overly sensitive listeners, victims of a heart-on-sleeve approach. To put it another way, when it comes to listening most of us seem somewhat "allergic," interpersonally speaking. There is something emotionally un-settling about the speaker or message—a physical mark, poor diction or grammar, an objection in sales, a strongly negative expression—that causes us to overreact.

These verbal jabs touch off a reaction. And the intensity of our reac-tions magnifies the flaw. (Compare road rage, plane rage, and workplace rage whereby a magnified emphasis on the negative warps perception and impairs one's judgment.) The listener, momentarily thrown off stride, then continues the conversation on autopilot, all the while mulling over the wound, smarting from the event's aftershocks.

These *star events* flash distraction and have the emotional potential to sidetrack our thinking. Catching us off guard, they push our emotions into overdrive, disrupting the receiving process. These are often the deflating moments that cause annoyance, frustration, anxiety, defensiveness, fear, or denial (but sometimes, even complacency). Viscerally offended by them, we quickly come under stress. We are then consumed by our personal turmoil, or tend to react and respond negatively or defensively.

Star events highlight the listener's emotional vulnerability (we may not yet have fully shed our defensive armor). As indictments taken personally, they test the limits of our ability to deal with them objectively. The mind then gets stalled as the speaker moves on. You can think of a star event as an emotional aneurysm: there is weakening, as in the wall of a brain artery, and a similar potential for ballooning (here, of emotions) if we don't do something to counteract the situation.

Consider, for example, an amateur baseball player who fouls off a pitch he knows he should have hit. While he's thinking about his mistake, he isn't ready for the next pitch. The road to listening is pitted with many such emotional reactions. During a listening exercise in one of my seminars, a participant actually found he could not understand what his partner was saying. They were discussing cable TV programming and censorship, and because he strongly disagreed with the speaker's point of view, he suffered blockage.

There are times when we may be expecting a particular response, and we don't get it (or we get something else). We all know how we feel when our favorite suggestion is dead-ended by a colleague or boss who says, "That's a good idea, but..." or uncharitably generalizes by saying, "All you (...) people are interested in is making a buck!" We find these and similar remarks irksome. They get under our skin.

How can we keep from capsizing emotionally? What can we do to counter these emotional winds that threaten to drive us off course? And how do we remove or distance ourselves from the unsettling currents left in their wake? *You can ward off distraction by heightening your own level of response.* Feedback can be a preemptive tactic, providing an anchor that tends to steady our focus by grounding us in the present. With feedback, the turmoil subsides.

Each of us has repetitive bouts with emotional distraction. Star events can be difficult, but they don't have to rule our listening. We don't have to take the brunt of distressing emotional upheaval. We can do something about it. Identify your own star events that trigger strong feelings in you. Learn to see them as a wake-up call that signals impending loss of focus, a prelude to losing concentration. Then counteract their effect by weighing in with a bit more responsiveness and feedback than you might normally do. By responding neutrally or feeding back, we can dodge the bullet or bounce back after a heavy punch.

Distortion

Speakers on the whole can be a lot clearer about what they really mean. But often we are tempted to hear what we want and expect to hear. And this further compromises our listening and understanding.

An associate and I once paid a sales call on three women. I thought the conversation was going rather well, when the woman in charge suddenly turned to me and said, "It's taken you fifty-five minutes to make a single reference to a woman!" I was shocked because I had gone out of my way to avoid this very reaction, having been sure to say things such as "to his advantage and to hers" and "to accomplish her goal and his." I appealed to my associate who said assuringly, "Yes, Dick did say that several times."

We hear what we need, want, or expect to hear. How many times have we paid only halfhearted attention to what another is telling us? Listening is an activity so often compromised by an overly casual ear. Misunderstandings happen. And inefficiencies have consequences. We may too hastily draw an inference or conclusion unless we discipline our minds to the message and involve our imaginations in the meaning it conveys.

Not too long ago, a training colleague of mine received a fax with the names of participants who had registered for his upcoming public workshop. Hoping that there would be sufficient enrollment to warrant holding the session, he was suddenly taken aback when he read the handwritten message on the second page: "I am sorry. There are only seven signed up." He assumed this was an apology for canceling the program. Only after calling the coordinator was he told, "It's a go." (The written message was only intended as regret that more people had not signed up for the course!)

Our expectations of what we think we're going to hear can create distortion and cause us to miss or misread the message. Listening is a labor-intensive effort. To follow the flow throughout the course of a conversation (or written communication) requires a steady alertness and mental agility.

Here again focus and feedback can ensure a close tracking in conversations and a certified record of shared communication. This is another reason why listening leaders check in frequently with their partners and respond early. They walk the line between what they expect to hear and what is actually said with grace.

Listeners would do well to keep their minds open to the evolving nature of the message (verbal or emotional). We must calculate and weigh and, if necessary, struggle not to hurry our time with the speaker.

Defensiveness

Beleaguered listeners must also learn to cope with their own defensiveness. When we feel under attack, our fundamental impulse is to get our armor up, to ward off what we perceive to be a threat to our position, authority, or point of view.

Suppose, for example, you are having a phone conversation with a prospective client. At one point, you ask a question, only to be asked in return: "Were you listening?" It can be hard to avoid getting on your high horse and protecting yourself. It's a tricky task to find a neutral response—to turn challenge into opportunity—so that we don't ... *willfully translate our insecurity and hurt into a prickly defensiveness.*

The problem with defensiveness is that it cuts off perception. It announces publicly that you have stopped listening, and few of us can afford that. The opposite of defensiveness is openness and honesty.

For example, a new receptionist confesses, "It's only my second day on the job." A salesman states with honesty, "You've caught me off guard." One admits to a certain vulnerability. Leaders have the supreme social virtue, for example, of owning up to a knowledge gap (either in subject matter or in the specific issue at hand).

We, too, can find within ourselves the courage and capacity to be more forthrightly candid: "I'm sorry. I guess I don't see how that experience relates to what you are telling me now." "Could you back up a step, and run that by me again?"

More often than not, however, we opt for a protective reaction or fire a return salvo: "Why are you singling me out?" "I wasn't the one who messed up on that project!" Our impetuous way with response behavior can lead us into a defensive stance, acting out defensive routines. Here follows a telling example.

I was in a taxi when the driver told me of an experience he had had in stopping for a woman passenger. It had been raining, and as she entered his cab, she promptly warned him, "Don't drive like a maniac!" Taking immediate offense, the driver replied, "Lady, I've been driving for twenty-seven years. You can get out now." As we discussed his reaction, I probed to see if he could see the situation from her viewpoint (admittedly, she used a poor choice of words). He couldn't. He felt his reputation, his ability, and perhaps his very manhood had been attacked. He wasn't going to stand for that! (Evidently, he felt he could afford to lose her as a customer; you and I might not feel that we could.)

When we put ourselves at the center of our listening, it is understandable why we so often mobilize for defense. For example, it is natural for parents to assume a protective posture if one of their children is sent home from school with a note for not doing a homework assignment or for misbehaving. They may take it as a personal affront, perhaps even going into denial. Now, suppose your teenage son hurls at you the accusation that "everything you do is hypocritical." What do you feel inside? How do you respond? Most of us would be hard-pressed to think quickly on our feet and come up with some form of neutral response.

But when listening is based on strategy, not reaction, cooler heads can prevail, and we can remain open. We can ask, "What makes you get that impression?" Why do you feel that way? "Would you be more specific?" Or in a different situation, "What would be the way you might prefer to approach the problem?"

Try another example. In asking your boss for a raise, he mentions a figure much lower than you expected. You might say, "That surprises me." Such a neutral response allows you to remain open and the discussion to continue. You and your boss may then have a better chance to negotiate a satisfactory agreement.

Putting our armor down may, at first, make us feel vulnerable. Ultimately, though, it fosters a more positive climate in which both parties can be more honest with each other.

Distraction, distortion, and defensiveness can cause rocky moments in listener–speaker togetherness. Left unchecked, they can become further constraints on achieving listening success. We can make peace with our inner demons by better understanding how we can strengthen focusing power and responsiveness.

PART 2

Motivational Listening

CHAPTER 4

Toward Conversational Continuity and Responsibility

As we spend longer hours in meetings, phone conversations, interviews, workshops, and selling situations, there is a greater urgency for more efficient, higher-profile listening. Yes, getting the message, but also managing effectively issues of relationship, feedback, rapport, and perceived commitment.

As we have seen, this is a difficult split in a listener's performance. We are expected to take in, process, and understand incoming information; and at the same time, we carry responsibility for letting it show. In other words, introspective concentration on one hand, outwardly expressive responding on the other. As we attend to the processing, we often neglect—or largely reduce—the other, presenting a blank demeanor that can discourage trustful sharing. A more open style propagates rapport.

The Concept of Articulate Listening

In spite of its unexpected name, the notion of articulate is a useful one around which to organize listening—in both aspects. Much of what passes for listening isn't really listening at all: it is *inarticulate*. And when listening is inarticulate, the mind's focus isn't nearly as sharp as it should be or can be; information is fuzzy; and relation and understanding are undisclosed. The result is parallel monologues that occasionally intersect, instead of true dialogue and mutual understanding.

A Definition

Articulate listening means raising what is heard to higher consciousness and externalizing the fact of being attentive. This term accurately expresses the significance of utilizing every available insight and tool to ensure full comprehension and sending back a "return receipt."

Often our unspoken position is "I got your message; just don't expect a reply." But processing alone is interpersonally inadequate. Conversation needs feedback and response to grow and prosper, and feedback is the collaborative component of the process.

When listening is articulate, points are clearer; ideas are more sharply defined; messages are more meaningful, more memorable; and there is more rapport in the relationship. Put simply, articulate listening is an efficiency tool for managing conversation. It is a method of streamlining the way we take in information and converting it into more productive connection. Clearly, this entails being dutiful not only to the message but also to the sender, listening not only to the problem but also to the person.

Most significantly, *articulate listening holds out promise of a new and more creatively entrepreneurial role for the listener, a role in which the listener takes the initiative in creating dynamic new connection opportunities and fuller understanding.* The thought-driven listener may yet become an interpreter of surprising warmth. But how do we hang tough in the face of ever-mounting information and increasing demands on our time? We can make our listening articulate, in part, through strategic feedback and response.

A Bridge to Influential Listening

Too many of us pass over the influential role feedback plays in conversation. We have been so conditioned by the narrow transmission model of the ideal listener that most of us don't have enough profile to be influential. Yet, by sometimes feeding back what you hear the speaker say, you can raise your visibility and have a larger presence, which makes you a significant player in the conversation.

Keep in mind that by making strategic use of feedback skills, we can have a far-reaching impact on the speaker, the relationship, and ourselves. In earlier examples, we saw how partnering with the speaker in this way helped manage the communication by focusing and clarifying meaning. Relating to what someone is saying also serves to transform a monologue into a discussion, while providing the rapport needed to keep the conversation flowing. And, just as important, we as listeners also benefit from such explicit expression by building self-confidence and stimulating within ourselves a solid sense of self-worth.

To manifest an affecting listening presence is an act of *influence*. This is not influence of the manipulative, self-seeking kind but rather a catalyst for positive change and goal realization. We execute with more authority. In this sense, listening can also be part of our capacity for personal projection.

As an articulate listener you can play a crucial enabling role, because your more open, inclusive style encourages others to give you more pertinent information. In selling, this means plugging into the pulse beat of buyers; in team management, this means surfacing hidden issues and providing a cohesive element to bring members closer together in pursuit of a common goal.

It has been said that leaders *get commitment from others by giving it themselves.* When we show our respect by fully listening to others, we can potentially motivate them to listen to us, to change, and to relate differently to us. This is the kind of style people are more likely to respond to. They get a good feeling about our sincerity and integrity. This is what listening leaders do: much more than passively registering incoming data, they actually *create and empower.*

A more influential, articulate listening style has a real payoff for managers and salespeople. Companies that promote and sell commercial products and services get closer to customers and grow stronger. Management organizations earn workers' respect and admiration and realize greater commitment and productivity.

But today salespeople and supervisors alike are too much at odds with themselves: they know they should be carefully listening for—and reflecting back—the customer's or associate's needs and concerns. Yet, too often they get caught up in the urgency to tell their own story (or set aright and provide the solution to the buyer's problem or the employee's dilemma). So they self-destruct. They don't want to listen; they want to talk.

They, too, must remember that feedback reconciles what appear to be contradictory demands. But, as we've noted, even then our uncertainty of when and how to interject a comment suppresses or forestalls feedback. When our pent-up reaction is finally released, it is late and its impact largely diluted.

The Key to Genuine Dialogue

When response and feedback are more freely given, the two parties play off each other, each serving as a mirror that reflects and adds dimension to the other. They alternately demonstrate their understanding to one another, becoming in the process kindred spirits in feeling and fact, interdependent and at ease in each other's company. Listener and speaker think and breathe as one.

The two together help shape the conversational agenda. Each party feels partnered by the other—neither has the sense of intruding on the other—and the conversation is the richer for it. The result is a gratifying high-efficiency, high-gain management-of-information exchange, which in turn generates goodwill and often gets the buy in.

That's why articulate-listening salespeople successfully differentiate themselves—and their products and services—in the minds of product-parity-perceiving buyers. Managers and supervisors who exhibit an articulate listening style line up with their subordinates in closely knit teams whose members individually feel more motivated to work *with* their bosses rather than *for* them. Both groups of professionals realize the higher returns of more respect, understanding, and cooperation.

To summarize: *Articulate listeners* successfully *parlay a keen sense of focus and involvement into two-part interplay.* Showing yourself to be a listening-ready leader will afford you a sounder basis for developing trustful relationships with your customers, subordinates, and coworkers. And all concerned will be motivated to work—or get into business—together.

Articulate listening takes some work, but it's worth the effort. Superior listening is a mark of distinction, an index of professionalism, and a hallmark of leadership.

Keeping the Speaker's Needs in Mind

As listeners we should ask ourselves: "How well do we perform against a speaker's expectations?" After all, speakers, like all entrepreneurs, invest their assets—message, intent, time, effort—and look for a reasonable return. This seems only fair.

But have you ever noticed how blankly unemotional our listening often seems? Our eyes make contact, but for stretches of time little else does. We bank heavily on the speaker's assuming that our direct gaze is the guarantee of our full presence. "I understand; I follow you," our style seems to say. True, a silent and deadpan demeanor may mask the fact that we are *indeed* paying attention. But for the rest, speakers are pretty much left to their imaginations.

When we're focusing on the message, we're usually not thinking about the speaker's needs. Few of us see a conversation through our partner's eyes. If we did, we might understand their perception of our maddening self-containment and impassivity, our seeming indifference. But we have all to do with just managing our side of the equation. To satisfy a speaker's concerns just doesn't seem part of the listener's job description. However, it is and for good reasons. Not unfairly put, speakers feel a sense of entitlement to speak their minds without incurring immediate rebuttal and to have their ideas acknowledged and their feelings validated.

What Does the Speaker Want from Me?

When we show ourselves to be in touch with others' emotions and needs, we create a much more efficient and mutually satisfying dialogue and relationship. So what do listeners owe their speakers? To answer this, we must look at listening from both sides now.

Imagine for just a moment that you are leading the conversation. It's you who are proposing a bright new idea to your boss or relating your frustration with some of the people on your work team. Scant output from your listener leaves you guessing almost everything about the situation. You try to pierce the inscrutable exterior of this very private person. But picking up barely a hint of intellectual fervor or emotional interest, you're puzzled, you feel unsure, you hesitate to go on, wondering whether the time and effort will be worth it.

Now you know how others feel when faced with a listener who seems, except in a few encouraging instances, to be distant and uninvolved: cheated, perhaps bruised, certainly unreciprocated. The feeling is one of talking to yourself, of living an unregarded existence.

It takes reminding that, by definition, conversation sets up certain expectations for the *speaker* as well as the listener, but does not always satisfy them. Typically, the speaker's message is less consummated than anticipatory. And the jolts of contrast between expectation and reality can be unsettling. Like most people, you and I alike seek connection and a shared sense of direction, but don't want to have to search for a listener's pulse to get it. We are more comfortable with, and drawn to, a listener who reacts and responds to us. When we disclose more of our listening, others tend to follow our example, which is a big payoff for little investment.

A paper industry engineer in one of my training programs once remarked to me, "You know, I always thought when you're listening, you just sit there. But when I think of the people I enjoy talking to—they're *expressive* listeners."

It's interesting that we would have speakers be expressive to hold our interest. But it works the other way as well.

Higher Returns from Listener Engagement

When a listener engages the speaker, it is a welcome and refreshing change. There is a powerfully felt immediacy: the listener is now here with me, having perhaps been somewhere else. Most speakers don't require or even expect boundless interest and curiosity; they are satisfied simply with less secrecy and a bit more sharing, an assist in comanaging the conversation and keeping it on center.

A phone call came in for my wife. She wasn't home at the time, so I took the message. Taking an interest, I wanted to satisfy the caller's need. Closely relating my responses to her request gave her the sense that I was trying to give her my full attention. This, in turn, was repaid with clear, coherent communication from the other side. And then I heard her say, "You're a good listener!" She felt satisfied (I was glad). There was closure.

A sense of agreeableness on our part registers strongly. The other person senses how closely you attend to the message. There is a sense of equal standing, of partnership. Our responsiveness gives testimony to the value we place on our partner and the conversation.

Listening is an astonishingly complex device, whose machinery is sealed from view and whose operation is not always certain—at least to the one talking. Speakers need clues to put their intellectual and emotional houses in order. The slightly more responsive listener can exercise real leadership in guiding the conversation, in helping the speaker improve message quality by being more specific or more forthcoming.

During a listening exercise in one of my workshops, a woman was relating to her partner an experience she had had. She later shared with the group her quite unexpected observation that her listener's feedback "focused my thinking."

The irony in much conversational listening is that the very speaker we are attending to may find the conservatism of our listening style unsettling. The stiffly starched listening style leaves us vulnerable to the charge of appearing smug and apathetic. And some speakers may feel isolated, frustrated, and betrayed. (Not to the same extent, but something like an inmate in a maximum security prison feeling that "prolonged isolation is the worst punishment you can put on a human being.")

An overly matter-of-fact listening style may also cause a speaker to hold back because he or she doesn't feel acknowledged and affirmed. As a listener, you will then have to work harder to get the information you may be seeking.

As with some fires, the noncommittal tone we sometimes set may be characterized by the speaker as suspicious. The famous contemporary concert violinist, Midori, was once quoted as saying, "I can only share when I am accepted by the person I am trying to share with." And just as a circuit tester is used to detect the presence of electricity, so, too, do speakers use the signs we give off to sense the extent of our listening activity, and to gauge the level of our interest and involvement.

Conversation is a braided cord of dialogue uniting speaker and listener in mutual interaction, and cannot be defined as a single action from mouth to ear. Therefore, *response* and *feedback* are not idle words to someone with a sense of the speaker's needs. An articulate listener knows to deliver the responses, the restatements, the feedback of ideas and emotions that inform a speaker that all is well on the other side. These listening indicators allow us to serve our partner like an attentive, sensitive accompanist at a song recital. Through these resources and tools, we can create conditions more conducive to conversational flow and authentic communication.

CHAPTER 5

Strengthening Focus

The listener's dilemma today can be put simply: faulty focus and restricted response. These two aspects of the process are not linked in the listener's mind, but they are intimately interrelated. If we are going to get more *out* of our listening, we need to know better what goes *into* it.

Containing Concentration

Let's begin by setting a systematic framework for thinking explicitly about the way we listen. We can break down the process into its strategic elements, categorizing them into two groups: (1) containment (controlling concentration) and (2) conscious convergence (connecting with the speaker).

The resourceful listener draws upon these two principal control factors to keep distraction at bay. *Containment* helps block out internal and external distractions, keeping concentration intact so the listener can be more receptive to spoken information. *Conscious convergence* then focuses this attention on the speaking situation at hand.

We all have concentration, but, like a temper, lose it sometimes. Focus is a fragile thing. We may, for a time, successfully focus on what someone is saying, but then distraction invades the mainstream of thought, and our mind runs off track.

What if we didn't have to put up with distraction? Suppose there were some way we could keep our mind from straying to other concerns.

Today, there are specially designed contact lenses that focus and intensify light. Unfortunately, we have nothing comparable for the ears that would keep our minds locked in to the message. But we can recognize certain focus risk factors—glitches that do the run-of-the-mill listener in—and turn them to our advantage. To contain concentration, we can look at the speaker, neutralize emotions, reposition the body, capitalize on thought speed versus talk speed, search for personal payoff, and look beyond verbal and visual appearance.

Eye Contact

It is estimated that we take in close to 90 percent of our face-to-face information today through the eyes. Looking at the speaker places him or her in a frame. Although not foolproof, this helps shift the percentages in the direction of success in staying focused. But don't make the mistake of making eye contact *to the point of unnerving fixation*. This can be too much of a good thing and backfire, by either being intimidating or causing eyestrain.

What's more, what is the operative word here? That's right, *contact*. And in a larger sense, that is what we should be concerned about in conversation: *creating and maintaining contact*.

Neutralize Emotions

As we proceed down the path of conversation, we may encounter an invisible barrier at any time. This can be anything we are hearing, seeing, or thinking—the *star events* we identified earlier—that hits a nerve (or, at least, touches an emotional chord). Something outlandish the speaker says grates our sensibilities. The other person's asking, "Why do you always make a big deal out of everything!" feels like a stab in the stomach. Or, you have just been asked the very question you feared, and you get down on yourself for not having a prepared answer. On the other hand, sometimes we can just as easily be lulled into complacency—we think "we have perfect agreement here"—and miss the fly in the ointment at the end.

Many of us are highly vulnerable to the emotional fallout of star events. These forces can then more easily bedevil our composure, poking our sore spots and setting us off. When we don't expect their visits, we are taken by surprise, caught off guard, and unhinged by them, leaving us little room for flexibility.

Although few are immune to the effects of these contagious viruses, the best listeners know to anticipate them. They then draw upon planned responses and are, thereby, less prone to sudden, unsettling disruption. By recognizing that these stressors are controllable and are, in a sense, self-inflicted wounds, these listeners then break the cycle by expanding awareness and personal options.

Most listeners need help responding to these mental spasms. Here are a few tips for all of us. First, recognize that poorly expressed, thoughtless remarks can cause you to lose control and self-destruct. You then become an angry combatant, instead of a communications partner. Strong listeners don't let these things get to them because *they are unwilling to let others have that kind of control over their behavior.*

Then get on intimate terms with your own emotional triggers, learn to expect them, and counter with a neutral response (as mentioned earlier in combating defensiveness). Suppose, for example, that a colleague or boss shoots down your proposal with "That's ridiculous!" You might respond with "What makes you feel that way?" Perhaps, "How would you suggest we address this particular issue?" Or possibly, "You must have some reason for saying that." Notice how such neutral responses allow the listener to shrug misgivings aside, maneuvering around the trouble spot. You don't have to dwell on feelings of resentment, rejection, or desertion. As with the training of airline pilots, *be prepared for any eventuality.*

The words from Anne Morrow Lindbergh's *Gift From the Sea* (1955, Pantheon) fit well here: "…how to remain whole in the midst of the distractions of life; how to remain balanced, no matter what centrifugal forces tend to pull one off center; how to remain strong, no matter what shocks come in."

So the next time social slights or indignities threaten to get under your skin and cause mental anguish, consider it a reminder to think: "I resent hearing those words. I'm about to lose focus if I am not careful. I must do something NOW." Then, without flinching, *keep your cool* and mental focus by countering with some unemotional response. Cooler heads and temperate thoughts must prevail to keep us from our natural instincts, and, with forethought and practice, they will.

At worst, star events sidetrack thinking, causing loss of focus and relationship. At best, they act as speed bumps that slow us down, or should give us pause.

Reposition the Body

As we listen to others and find our minds beginning to drift, we can rouse ourselves from our passivity by shifting, or reorienting, part or all of the body. For example, we can sit up straighter in our chair, or we can change our leg position so that both feet are on the floor. These physical movements—like the replacement of a foot that has gone to sleep—have the effect of increasing blood flow through a change in body position or angle. The repositioning need not be intrusive, but serves to "stir the sediment" and allows us to refocus anew.

Thought Speed versus Talk Speed

Sometimes in conversation we lag behind the speaker, caught up and swept along by star events or other distractions. When focus falters, we are off-line and momentarily out of the moment.

Often, though, we are one or two beats ahead of the speaker. This is because the mind operates faster than most of us speak (three to four times faster, in fact). Unskilled listeners use this differential to plan what they want to say next, indulge personal fantasies, or tune out altogether. Articulate listeners are aware of the disparities between mental comprehension and verbal output, whereby the mind often speeds to an end before the words driving it have run their course. These listeners don't consider this downtime, but *excess capacity*. They will use these spare moments to listen for completion; mentally take stock; note the choice of words, the set of the face, and the use of the voice; check their understanding; or offer some other appropriate response.

Search for Personal Payoff

Speakers rarely seem more boring than when they are engaged in rarified reasoning and discoursing on some overly technical topic. It can be slow going for those of us not absorbed by such subjects, and it can severely test listeners' goodwill.

That said, it can still pay to be an opportunist. Time is short. If I am really serious about elevating my listening performance and professionalism as a communicator, I will want to capitalize on every opportunity.

Good and bad examples of listening abound everywhere. We simply do not sharply identify them much of the time. For example, at your next meeting try to make a point to deliberately focus on the *objective*. Challenge yourself to uncover what it is and how well the discussion relates to it. Encourage yourself to listen through until you have. Or, make a conscious effort to observe how people listen during question-and-answer exchanges. Catch someone doing something right, and identify what it is. (You will probably also notice poor practices you will want to avoid.)

Try following the lead of high-performing listeners who have a knack for finding relevance in less than overtly relevant events. By redefining the reality of your situations so that they yield more value for you, you will be making better use of your time. And you will be using the occasion to spur yourself further along your personal path to improved listening.

Look beyond Verbal and Visual Appearance

We have already acknowledged the need to be *discerning* in our perceptions and *discriminating* in our judgments. But listeners who do not quite respect the person in front of them have a way of drifting into private ruminations.

Let's not forget that the present is shaped and measured by the past. People at either end of the conversation have trouble seeing beyond their own perspectives. We are hardly aware that our perceptions have tinted the windows through which we gaze out at others. Nor do we realize the extent to which we are in the grip of our own feeling at the moment and at the mercy of our own experience.

Repetitive situations present a special kind of challenge. Perhaps especially in business, listeners must learn to cope with their continuous and unrelenting exposure to the same or similar problems or situations. Familiarity becomes numbing, the originality fading into half-attended background talk. We may have heard it all before. A good example is the internist who has seen a hundred viral throat colds in the winter season. When you see him about yours, he must be careful to listen very closely so that you don't feel that he's giving you and your condition short shrift. Otherwise, you may be inclined to take your business elsewhere. (Keep in mind that, although a matter may be "old hat" to *you*, some people—in any given situation—may *be asking a question or presenting a problem for the first time.) We must strive to get past ourselves* to be fair-minded in our judgments.

And what we see depends on where we look and how it is illuminated—whether literally by light or figuratively by information. I remember once noticing, for the first time, a neighbor's front lawn as it was just being relandscaped: small, planted trees and shrubs vastly overshadowed by immense rocks. It looked to me grotesquely bare and disproportionate at the time. But as the weeks and months passed, and the landscape filled in, the scene took on greatly enhanced beauty and balance. The formerly oversized rocks had become background to the growing trees and shrubs. Everything now blended in together symmetrically. And I realized I had been hasty in my first evaluation.

We often judge too quickly, before needed information is provided that will complete the picture and force a reappraisal. If we remain complacent, or continue to rationalize, we remain boxed in by bias. We set ourselves up as the supreme arbiter, missing vital facts and nuances we may need to make the right decision or reach the right conclusion.

Although we may sometimes worry about being negatively influenced by the thinking of others, words of truth should be embraced no matter their origin. Let's remember that we are often quick to judge a statement, not on its own merits, but by its source. The credibility of an opinion often has more to do with who said it than with its content. Certainly the reputation, or our perception, of the speaker is one of the factors we use when we determine the value of what we hear. However, relying excessively much on the authority of particular speakers—without rigorously analyzing the contents of their statements—"... can lead us to become lazy and imprecise in our own thinking and decision-making." We can absorb and reflect back without necessarily having to assimilate to the views and feelings of others.

The Combined Power of Containment Tools

To capture success, you have to have the right focus and be in the moment. (Lynn Harrell, the renowned cellist, once commented in a New York Times music review about the inimitable artistry of the legendary violinist Jascha Heifetz: "When you see a film of Heifetz playing, you see a concentration and ferocity of intense living-in-the-present.") By working to achieve a cool, detached objectivity, we set up the possibility that relevant information can enter a more receptive mind. Also in writing a novel, one must develop a temperament that accepts concentration over the long haul. So, too, with listening.

Containment tools provide a reassuring framework for controlling mental clutter and distraction by converting them into focused concentration.

They keep our minds from wandering and put us on a higher state of alert. Following the flow of a speaker's narrative requires such alertness, undiluted by overheated moments or ungenerous—if not inaccurate—assessments. This strategic state of readiness then prepares us for the next step—to connect with the speaker by letting our listening show.

CHAPTER 6

Spanning the Communicational Divide

If staying focused is one challenge facing today's listeners, finding a distinctive voice is another. Like the average speaker, ordinary listeners make no apparent effort to cultivate a reassuring contact.

Occasional brief bits of sound are forthcoming as we make fleeting cameo appearances. But essentially we as listeners are silent, strangely hidden figures. At times, we even drop out entirely, leaving the unaccompanied speaker to convey the substance and mood of the conversation unaided.

Our inactions can build a wall around us, distancing us from others. Failing to take advantage of strategic responding, we forfeit our ability to reconcile differences, to assuage a speaker's anxieties. Just as bad, we are more prone to distraction. Elements of information may then fail to register, leaving gaps in the message. On the other hand, we hear more clearly for having temporarily connected with our speaking partner.

Connecting with the Speaker

Clearly, the act of taking in information must be balanced against the purpose of the conversation and the speaker's interpersonal needs. And so the next step is to actually connect with the speaker *by more fully disclosing our listening*. Remember, as speakers we all have a strong need to feel fully received and understood. That's why top-notch listeners in conversation know to serve not only as accompaniment to solo speakers but also as potent partners in their own right. They realize that feedback replaces the detached, autonomous individual with a collaborative partner and team player, thus consummating the relationship. And here is a great paradox of great listeners: In disclosing more aspects of their own personalities, they reveal more aspects of the speaker's. When we feed back, we often draw similar effort from others. So these listeners hover between the private sector and the public domain: a rare balance of aptitudes.

But how can we engage the speaker? The deeper question is, How can we make the most of our time in conversation? Here, of course, we are in the traditional area of feedback skills, or what we may call *convergence techniques* (if we don't converge with the speaker, we diverge). We can make a deliberate effort, a *conscious convergence*, to direct (or redirect) our thinking outward toward the message and our conversation partner. This explicit disclosure of our listening (feedback) builds and solidifies the relationship because it shrinks the distance between us. Feedback has the value of not only rekindling interest in both parties but also restoring a human dimension to conversation. Leaders are more successful when they generously spike their listening with responsiveness. As you work to cement your own hold on these resources, remember that you are thus demonstrating a leader's more effective stewardship of the listener role. This in turn will boost your influence and leadership profile.

To consciously converge, we can:

- react responsively,
- summarize out loud,
- paraphrase content,
- ask clarifying questions,
- take notes,
- reflect feelings, and
- read between the lines.

React Responsively

The surest way to give evidence of our listening is to respond. Responding is *reacting* in some way to something the speaker says. Responding has the effect, too, of refocusing our attention in case our minds have momentarily wandered off in search of more stimulating fare. We sometimes respond bodily—as in a head nod, change of eye contact, facial expression, hand gesture, or body movement—or in words.

Responding may simply serve as a request to have the question or statement repeated. For example: "Could you run that by me again?" Or: "You lost me there." More often, our responding simply indicates that we have received what was said. So, for example, we tend to use generalized and vague responses such as "yeah," "right," "hmm," "mhm," or "uh-huh." These minimal markers help regulate the conversation, yet carry little or no emotional value. On occasion, we may even ratchet up our personal involvement and say things such as "interesting," "I can imagine," "really?" "is that right!" "you're kidding!" "wow!" "it's true." And then there are times when a listener's more imaginative response engenders a feeling of closer relationship.

Training Manager (discussing the prospect of using outside training): We've done two rounds of training, but the third round has had to be put off a few months because of a softening market. At least we have the commitment. In past years, training would have been cut.

Training Consultant: Well, at least THAT'S encouraging!

Or:

Author (discussing my writing of this book with a friend): The notion of responding as being influential and motivating takes listening and the listener to a whole new plane.

Friend: That's what you're doing as I'm listening to you. You're taking me to a whole new plane.

These more specific response forms tend to stimulate rapport. More direct and meaningful, such comments demonstrate our higher interest level and signify that communication has taken place.

More affecting types of response also include summarizing out loud, paraphrasing, asking clarifying questions, reflecting underlying feelings, and reading between the lines. These are effective ways of feeding back all or part of what was heard for the purpose of confirming or correcting certain information, or identifying with the speaker. We need to rediscover the appeal—and *influence*—of feedback, and how to give it, if we're going to gain more respect and forge closer bonds with prospects and customers, colleagues and coworkers, friends and acquaintances.

Summarize Out Loud

Let's consider an example of summarizing out loud:

Sales Coordinator: You know, I'm still wondering about this new flyer. It's not clear to me how it adds value to what we already have. And what real sales use does it have? Besides, how large a selling role should it play?

Sales Associate: I think I really hear three concerns you seem to have, Linda. First, how does this promotional piece add anything new? Second, how can it be used with customers? And finally, how much should we rely on it in the actual selling situation? Is that right?

Sales Coordinator: Yes, that's it.

Here is another example of summarizing:

Administrative Assistant: So if I have it right, you want me to prepare a draft of the proposal, include the group's suggestions from today's meeting, and have it on your desk by tomorrow morning?

Boss: Exactly.

Paraphrase Content

Closely related to summarizing is paraphrasing a speaker's content. This means to rephrase or restate in your own words—as objectively as you can—what you think you heard the speaker say. When you paraphrase, you retrace the message, trying to capture the original. This is the ability to grasp meaning whole and to emit it intact. Restatement is like a re-telling of a story, only stripping the message to its narrative bone. By checking out what you think you heard against what was said, you can reduce, as far as possible, any discrepancy in meaning.

This is, after all, what a good consultant does. Coming into a new situation, he or she must determine what the client's problem is and come up with a specific and realistic solution. The client's explanation may contain considerable extraneous information (low signal-to-noise ratio) that obscures the matter. Listening attentively—and using paraphrasing to work through successive approximations—the consultant ultimately identifies the issue and focuses it.

Here is another example of paraphrasing:

Supervisor: Dave, I'm having a problem with the way you phrased this section of the report. I'm having trouble understanding just what you mean.

Associate: You mean the particular choice of words here is not getting the point across for you?

Another example:

Manager: In this particular area, we've gone from the general to the specific.

Associate: Sort of like, in advertising, moving from mass marketing to precision targeting?

Manager: Yes, something like that.

Notice how paraphrasing helps you, the listener, manage the speaker's talk by focusing it more sharply and achieving a common frame of reference. The immediate past is revisited by reading over the speaker's shoulder, so to speak, and information is certified. These overt attempts on your part to capture accurately what was said clear up potential misunderstanding, and the meaning of information—once clarified—is more easily assimilated. In addition, restatement also serves, as do other forms of feedback, to intensify the message for better recall.

Ask Clarifying Questions

Another effective way to shed more light on something said is to pose questions intended to clarify the meaning or situation. This helps the speaker increase message value by adding information or being more precise. It serves to remind that what was said was not necessarily obvious and meaningful to the listener. In turn, the listener indicates his or her honest effort to capture the true meaning of the message. Note the use of clarifying questions in the following example.

Supervisor: I'm a little surprised, frankly, that those percentages are so high.

Team Leader: Can you be more specific? What exactly surprises you?

Another example:

Sales Manager: I've asked you in this morning, Nancy, to talk about your job performance to date. You know, you started off so well, and showed signs of being one of our high-potential managers. And now, there's been a marked drop-off over the last few weeks. How do you account for that?

Sales Associate: Yeah, I know. Well, when I began, things seemed to be coming together real well. Then there were some changes, and that's when all the problems began.

Sales Manager: When you say, " 'all the problems," what do you mean? [Or, perhaps, What sort of problems?]

Sometimes, picking up on a particular word or phrase, we can play it back ("echoing") to the speaker for further clarification. This is illustrated in the last example and in the following:

Supervisor: Unfortunately, when she first started working for me, I was away on vacation.

Consultant: Unfortunately?

Supervisor: Yes, because the other woman gave her a hard time.

It is characteristic of some listeners to pose many of their questions so that a simple yes or no answer will suffice. For example, "Did you like the speaker?" "Do you feel she went behind your back?" "Are you finding any differences on your new job?"

The way these questions are formulated allows the respondent to provide only a short answer and little information. Note how the phrasing of the following *open-ended* version of these questions requires more thoughtful responses and elicits more meaningful information: "How will you use the information provided by the speaker?" "Why might you feel she went behind your back?" "What differences are you finding on your new job?" (Open-ended questions often, but not always, begin with a question—words such as *what, why, how, where,* or *when.*)

When you ask such clarifying questions, you're not interrogating the speaker. They are not so much demands, but requests. The speaker normally will not feel defensive. On the contrary, this tactic tends to increase the flow of conversation, allowing the speaker to give more specific, useful information.

Often overlooked, though, is this hugely important truth: A question can also be more than a device for gaining further information; as an interactive tool, it can bond you to others so that they do not feel isolated.

What we see, so far, is that a listener's performance is incomplete and woefully inadequate when either attending or responding alone carries most of the load. Listeners who combine feedback with focus—and complement collaboration with concentration—demonstrate a goodwill commitment to foster fuller understanding and relationship. Then all parties to a conversation can expect more positive results to follow.

Now, let's consider what else is needed to make contact with speakers.

Take Notes

Note taking is a familiar and easy way to preserve information. Often, we will jot down these written reminders to ourselves while reading or thinking. But taking brief targeted notes while in a conversation can also serve the purpose of making contact with the speaker and showing your genuine level of interest in what you are hearing.

People sometimes say that taking notes distracts them from listening to the full message. After clarifying how they are managing this shorthand tracking system, it may turn out that they are not going about things in the most efficient way. If you are one of these people, perhaps you are taking too many notes or maybe not the right kind of notes. Is it possible that, while engaged in this process, you lose sight of the simultaneous need to keep contact with the speaker through verbal or nonverbal feedback?

You might find an *oscillating* process helpful when taking notes. That is, first determine the overall purpose of the discussion (or presentation). Then take down some specifics. However, don't remain at only the level of individual points but step back and assess the underlying theme. Then, listen again for specific details. I find that this moving in and out, relating parts to wholes, gives me a chance to define a framework in which particular events have meaningful relationships. Put differently, in most cases this process will enable you to appreciate individual points while keeping the larger picture in view.

As you take notes during a conversation, try to remember to look up from time to time to regain eye contact. At the same time, you can offer a comment, or ask a question, while your finger keeps the place in your notes. So we see that engaging the speaker while taking notes does not necessarily have to derail our efforts to fully listen. Yes, it may well take practice. But like properly balancing inbound and outbound listening, it is possible to juggle these two efforts successfully by keeping your written reminders short and to the point.

Of course, any system of note taking is only as good as the time you take, soon after, to review what you have written down. Here is where many people fail to follow through. It only makes good sense to revisit your notes as soon after the event as possible, so that you can reconstruct your jottings while they are still fresh in your mind and complete the record of your experience.

A double benefit results. While you were jotting down certain points and details in the speaker's message, the speaker was also taking note of your obvious involvement in the conversation and intent to capture essential aspects of your exchange.

Reflect Feelings

Now we come to dealing with feelings. Feelings are worth thinking about because they can often either get in the way of clear communication and understanding or be used positively to build the relationship.

That notwithstanding, we tend to be overly cerebral. Although most of us will grant that we all think and feel, and would agree that another's feelings are as genuine as our own, we tend to be more attuned to the rational realm of ideas. Sadly, many of us have come to deny not only our own feelings but others' as well. And time and again, for most listeners, the speaker's emotions are a peripheral event.

My wife had been working for about fifteen years as a learning disabilities specialist in the elementary grades. Every day she would meet outside the regular classroom with individual children needing extra help in certain subjects so that they could catch up and be mainstreamed with the rest of their class.

One day, she confided to me: "You know, I would love someday to have a classroom all to myself." Sometime later, after we had both arrived home after a hectic day at work, we were standing in the kitchen when she exclaimed: "Guess what! In September, I'm going to be completely in charge of a first-grade class!"

Feeling tired, with my personal response system down, I simply replied, "Great," and walked into the living room. Suddenly, hearing that hollow response in my head, I stopped short and thought to myself: "Uh-oh, I think I can do better than that." Walking back into the kitchen, I said (somewhat apologetically), "You know, Estelle, now that I stop and think about it, that's something you've been looking forward to for such a long time. You must really feel *wonderful!*" Beaming, she said, "I really do."

I had now managed to connect with her on an emotional level. (Hearing this, one workshop participant wryly remarked, "You probably saved your marriage!") No, I'm not a hero in this story. But it does show how we can catch ourselves. We can find on-ramps, ways to log back on to do better justice to our partner and the conversation.

A listener may be engaging to talk with, but oddly lacking in emotional resonance. Just because you are physically close to your partner—and understand the words—doesn't mean you are in the same area code emotionally. We may not even *hear* the signals of expression; or, hearing them, not really *feel* them; or, finally, feeling them, not actually *reflect* them. And this is not something new. The eighteenth-century English author Oliver Goldsmith observed: "People are generally calm at others' misfortune."

Why is this? Why do listeners, on the whole, show so little evidence of an *emotional persona*? Are we simply too caught up in ourselves? Perhaps. But this emotionally barren style also probably stems from a combination of bottom-line thinking and an unconscious attitude that says that to be concerned with emotion is somehow irrelevant to the supposedly non-intuitive demands of listening. But cognitive relations alone is a limited partnership: there may be intellectual communion, but little or no emotional satisfaction. Consider the following situation.

You are a salesman. And you have tried numerous times to get a prospect on the phone. Each time, you get a busy signal. Finally, on the tenth try, you get through and tell the secretary, "I haven't been able to get through all day!" The secretary, seemingly numb to your frustration, casually explains, "We've been having trouble with our phones." There is no apology, no validation of how you must feel. However, once you understand what the problem was, you could—if you wanted to—try redirecting the focus and say empathetically, "Oh, that must be a hardship for you." This tactic sets a positive example and leaves open a relationship you may wish to continue.

A speaker's message may include important emotional information—the way he or she feels about what is being said. But these indicators of mood tend to slip under our radar if we are a "just-the-facts, Ma'am" receiver. Now, wait a minute, you say. "What is this? Some saccharine sentiments? New-world wimpiness? I don't have time to play the therapist!" No, it's not, and no, you don't. We're talking about listening that appeals not only to the head but also to the heart. And even in these seemingly harsh days, people have hearts to be touched. That's why one danger in interpreting a message is to process only the words, and then to dismiss the emotion as self-indulgence.

A participant in one of my seminars once shared this experience: He got into a discussion with a fellow town resident who was dissatisfied with a certain elected official. Over time, the discussion became adversarial, and this participant didn't know why. Subsequently, he came to realize that he had been listening to the other fellow *"exclusively on the word level*, and had greatly underestimated the man's frustration."

This clearly illustrates what can happen when we fail to read a speaker's mood due to an excessively narrrow intellectual focus. Like a composer who died in a given year but whose musical career keeps growing, so too a speaker's words define, *but the meaning is larger*. There is more truth to discover. Think of interactions in the family, performance appraisals, the coaching of subordinates, training sessions, and other situations in which sensitivity dictates that we also pay close attention to the texture of the message and make an emotional connection.

Some speakers have a need for emotional validation. This means *feeling along*, as well as thinking along, with them. Could a speaker's emotion—pride, ownership, uncertainty, frustration, commitment, comfort, confidence, fear, anger or defensiveness—at least be granted some marginally detectable blip on our seismograph?

I once overheard this segment of a radio talk show:

Guest: I'm about to retire after forty-two years at the same company.

Interviewer: Really.

The interviewer could have shown more sensitivity and interest in the guest's tacit expression of personal pride. For example, he might have replied with something like "That's great. How many people can say that!" No, we don't have to agree with a feeling to show that it is registering on our personal Richter scale. Nor does such emotional acknowledgment need to be verbal: emotion on the face often speaks louder than words. But empathy usually goes a long way toward bringing two or more people closer.

Martha Manning, reviewing two books by psychotherapists in the October 31, 1997, *New York Times* book review section, wrote that "Empathy is not simply some magical capacity to intuit another's feelings. Rather, it is a dynamic process, involving two people's ability to express their thoughts and feelings to each other in ways that add, change and, most important, *continue* the relationship."

Indeed, in previous chapters we saw that feedback and response can provide the impetus to lift the dialogue right out of its normal context and let a new relationship form. All too often, though, our experience of the message is fragmented and fragmentary at best. We take in and use limited signals from the person in front of us without letting other signals penetrate as well. Prolonged silence in the face of these may be read as apathy or indifference. Such silence weakens the potential bond. Yet self-esteem is a potent concern for anyone, and emotion cannot be denied.

By tracking signals of voice, face, and body, a pursuing listener can go beyond the words to home in on the more personal aspect of the message. When listening is emotionally effective, we display an ability to smooth ruffled feelings, to diffuse negative emotions, to reduce stress. A speaker feels safe enough to be more open and honest. And, once again, we are being influential.

In an interview with a flight attendant reported in The New York Times Sunday Travel section, when she was asked how she dealt with unruly passengers, she said: "I've never had a passenger be rude to me. I find that putting myself in other people's shoes gets me through 99 percent of any problems. If a passenger has a complaint, I look them in the eye and ask, 'If you were in my position, what would you expect me to do for you?' They usually say: 'Nothing. I just needed someone to listen.' People need to vent."

To capture mood as well as substance requires expanding our focus to process the incoming message on not just one, but two tracks—the verbal (or cognitive) and the emotional—and analyzing each on its own terms. This brings heightened rapport and greater accuracy than an undifferentiated approach that does not distinguish between thoughts and feelings.

The sensitive listener proves to be an empathetic partner. The style is deeper, subtler, more individual, and unexpected. Which leads one to wonder: *Do listeners sense a speaker's mood and evade acknowledging it*, or *do listeners not sense what a speaker's mood is? Can any sense of the empathic be taught to those who lack it instinctively?*

My experience in training others to listen and speak effectively demonstrates that one can also learn to be a more feeling communicator. Fuller awareness of another's needs, ample practice in emotional acknowledgment, and a keenly felt sense of personal payoff engender a stronger motivation and commitment to connecting on this level.

To help you develop a more vivid ear and become more astute in detecting emotional meaning, consider the following examples. Note in each case how the listener reflects, or validates, the speaker's expressed feelings.

Worker: Hey, guess what? I just got a bonus!

Friend: Great! I'll bet this makes you feel terrific!

Another example:

Employee: Say, Bill. How's it going?

Colleague: Oh, I don't know. Everything seems to be piling up on me. I just lost my secretary, now they've dumped a new project on me with an unbelievable deadline, and I've just learned that I'm stuck with a bunch of summer interns I'm responsible for.

Employee: You've got some full plate, there! I can see why you seem so overwhelmed.

Many of us are used to listening at ground level (bottom line). We've been trained that way. Our immediate superiors expect us, after all, to attend closely to work-related details, problems, and issues. Throughout our careers, we are esteemed and promoted based on our capacity to understand and deal with a complex, ever-expanding array of increasingly technical facts and relationships. This focus seems objective, practical, and hard core, whereas emotions seem subjective, self-indulgent, and soft. It is hardly surprising, therefore, that we're more attuned to the rational than the emotional. But going beyond cataloging what happened to the person—to reflecting the states of mind and heart when they were happening—is not being indulgent or sentimental. *It's being an empathic professional* (and empathy is coming to be recognized as a personal success factor in leadership).

Sometimes, situations will require that we also get off the ground (above the bottom line) if we are to take the full measure of a message or situation. This is especially true in sales, team management, and performance appraisals, in which *unacknowledged* concerns can foster mistrust and inhibit communication.

Sporting a T-shirt with the words "I can empathize" on the front doesn't cut it, not by a long shot. People can tell that we in fact care only by our conduct, by the way we relate—or don't—to what they are saying and feeling.

Trying to achieve most things without a sense of solidarity isn't a strategy; it's wishful thinking. Although we are not psychologists, counselors, or members of the clergy, we can hear, and listen to, words fraught with fear and frustration. We can overcome unintended emotional remoteness. It is within our grasp, and strategically desirable, to develop more highly tuned radar for mood signals. It's a matter of cultivating an awareness of this other reality—this emotional dimension of meaning—and of how we can accomplish our goals more easily when we deal with emotional messages more effectively.

Read between the Lines

No discussion of making listening contact with others can be complete without addressing the crucial matter of *deciphering the code*, of figuring out what someone may REALLY be saying.

Often, perhaps more than we realize, people seem unable, or unwilling, to tell us what they truly mean. Some messages are straightforward; others can pose interpretive problems. This requires us to read between the lines, to track the true intent of what is meant, to get inside the facts, to uncover the suppressed thought or hidden motivation.

We are not altogether unfamiliar with this fact of listening life. It crops up in all kinds of interactions—in every field and in everyday living. In medicine, some doctors know that patients do not always come right out and say what is wrong. Sometimes, they hedge or obfuscate, and often the key to treating them is to look a little deeper. In education, use of the phrase "standards-based reform" is potentially ambiguous. It may refer to *minimum standards*, what all students must know for promotion or graduation; or it may mean high standards toward which all students should strive, but which they may not achieve. And the successful applicant for a job listens for the concerns behind the interviewer's questions.

The familiar "Do I detect a tone of sarcasm in your voice?" suggests our occasional awareness of this. As does common experience with utterances such as "Can you pass the salt?" (at a meal) and "I'm going to need your card" (when making a purchase)—both of which *imply a request* and are not intended simply to check your ability or to make a factual statement.

Generally, though, too many of us insist on taking the message literally. We conclude too quickly that the message possesses no depth to penetrate and so decide to deal with its surface, skimming meaning off the top. We forget that spoken messages can have complexities, nuances, and under-the-surface stories.

Here is an interesting example. How might you interpret the following statement? "I was out for a little while." It may be a wrong take on the message to read it as I went to the corner store (or to see a neighbor). Depending on context, it could mean that the speaker was unconscious (asleep or away from the job), or his mind wandered.

Because we are capable of meaning more than we say in words, it is possible to misread the message by a wide margin. We sometimes have to dig deeper and more purposefully to distill the core meaning. It can be frustrating and, at times, nigh impossible to tell where a speaker is coming from. And some people may consciously wish to deny or hide aspects of their messages, as in negotiations. (But we're not talking about strategic ambiguity, in which such a deliberate strategy might well work in quelling the anguish before it escalates and before true intent is revealed.)

We've seen how easy it is to get wrapped up in oneself and miss part or all of the message. It is also easy to get caught up in WHAT a speaker is saying and lose sight of HOW or WHY he or she is saying it. (How nice it would be if speakers provided a letter of intent along with the message, as corporations do at the time of takeover. But it's *our* job to sometimes dig a little deeper.) Consider the following example:

Subordinate: Well, I did what you *told* me.

Manager: And did it work?

A casual reading of the subordinate's message may miss an implied layer of resentment. A more perceptive, and welcome, response might then be: "It sounds as though you may not have been totally pleased with the results." This reflects a sensitive concern with the worker's attitude and keeps the relationship open.

Often, the most innocent, brief message may be colored with an underlay of emotion or personal meaning (much as in opera, in which the music reveals a subtext that works on a deeper level than the plot). A message, for example, such as "I have wide experience with that" can imply a world of heavy-duty circumstances behind it. (We saw this earlier, when I failed to read the implied meaning of those words while relating my first experience with a singles group to an editor of a magazine for singles!)

Now consider this example:

Workshop Participant: Do you really *believe* that?

Workshop Leader: It sounds as though you may have some doubts.

One could have read this question as a simple request for a yes or no answer. Here, sensing another meaning behind the message, the leader instead tries to tease out the underlying intent to distill a clear understanding. Articulate listeners probe every nuance, burrowing under and around the spoken word to extract the core meaning. The casual listener often fails to discern a speaker's attitude.

Here is another example:

One time, in a training program I was facilitating about persuasive presentations, the discussion turned to the question of personalizing presentations. One of the participants asked, "Can you ever be too personal?" Again, one might be tempted to answer with a simple yes or no, supported by further remarks. But on this occasion, I thought to myself: he's talking about personalizing presentations, but he really seems to be saying more than that. So I replied, "It sounds as though you feel there are times when you *can* be" (i.e., too personal). The discussion then proceeded in a more open and honest fashion than it might otherwise have.

The following example points up, once again, how easy it is to mistakenly harvest the message's husk and leave the kernel meaning behind.

Major health management organizations today may encounter this question from prospective subscribers: How many American doctors are in your physician network? This inquiry's underlying intent may be severalfold: What is the ethnic representation? What is the quality of medical care? Will my doctor know my language? And there could also be other possible interpretations. Only through probing can one be sure of the intended meaning.

While I was having a prescription filled in a local pharmacy, I happened to observe the following unexpected exchange between the pharmacist and a customer:

Pharmacist: You ever get anything from a health food store?

Customer (opening his jacket and revealing his heavy build): Yeah, you can really tell I do. (attempt at humor)

Pharmacist: It doesn't make any difference. I was asking because we're thinking of stocking some health food products in the store.

Taking the question personally, and perhaps feeling somewhat self-conscious, the customer had opted to joke about the situation, rather than try to discern the pharmacist's purpose in asking.

There is real meaning, and there is what the listener hears. The choice is ours whether to grasp the "plain" meaning (a surface orientation) or to try to penetrate a message's most interior meaning.

A friend of mine was recently a guest of honor at a local organization's annual dinner. We had the following exchange:

Author: Say, David, congratulations on your honor the other night.

Friend: It was a fund-raiser.

Author: You mean, they had to give it to *somebody*?
Friend: Yeah, I really didn't do anything.

Here, my friend's words intimated a larger truth.

There are also times when we may interpret a message in a light far different from the one the speaker wanted to throw on it. I recall that after completing a training workshop at an out-of-state motel, I approached the front desk and asked the director of marketing if I could leave my suitcase behind the counter for about an hour. "Certainly," she replied, and then asked, "by the way, how did it go?" Assuming she was referring to my workshop, I said, "I thought it went rather well. Everyone seemed to be involved and to enjoy the experience." As I walked off into the lobby, I suddenly stopped. It then occurred to me: I don't think that's what she was asking me. Immediately turning around, I went back to her. "Excuse me," I said, "but I have the feeling you may have been asking me something else. She smiled knowingly. I then realized that, as the director of marketing, she would naturally be more concerned about how pleased I was with the facilities, than with how my workshop went.

The lesson I took away from this example was that there are times when the matter of importance is not only WHAT is said or HOW something is said but also WHO is saying it. For example, whether the other person was in financial services or informational technology, you would do well to interpret matters in his or her frame of reference. One day, after my wife came home from a day of teaching, we had this memorable exchange:

Wife: I had to meet with parents during my prep time.
Author: So you really didn't have any time for yourself.
Wife: No.

By peeling back the layers, we can bring out some of the hidden meaning in a message that can seem to have said all it had to say.

In a similar way, the next example is revealing. The newspapers reported the sudden firing of a popular coach of a major college basketball team. A reporter interviewed a fan to get his reaction:

Fan: I think their letting him go like that was a big mistake.
Reporter: You mean, you feel they might have overreacted?
Fan: Absolutely!

The reporter successfully penetrated to the core import of the fan's words.

A few years ago, about the time hurricane Andrew devastated parts of the state of Florida, I happened to meet an older friend of mine in a local supermarket. We had the following brief conversation about hurricanes:

Friend: Have you ever been in a hurricane?

Author (with an automatic, knee-jerk reaction): No, fortunately! (then, searching his face, and replaying in my mind the voice tone accompanying his question) But it almost sounds like you may have been.

My friend then went on to tell me of the harrowing experience of his having lived through a hurricane.

Does one have to be gifted to read between the lines? No, but we see that it helps to remember that spoken utterances can be complex events, and one can even find implications in what is not said. As in some plays, "The weight of the scene is carried nonverbally."

Admittedly, there can be times when one seems to be looking too hard for meaning that isn't there. One might suppose that the quest for underlying meaning could get one into interpretive trouble. But this need not be the case. We are more likely to be dogged literalists than to read too much into what someone is saying.

Listeners today often mistake a message's surface meaning as being all there is. But to operate on the surface is sometimes to be shallow. Some utterances deserve closer attention. "Straightforward" messages may arrive with the baggage of multiple meanings. Influential listeners are alert to the possibility of larger meaning.

Remember, utterances "throw shadows." We are capable of meaning more than we say, giving off intimations of intention. Be alert to innuendo, insinuation and other forms of indirect communication by addressing the why and the how, as well as the what of the message. Then test your hunches. One clarifying approach might be to ask: "Do I understand that ...?" Or, "Correct me if I'm wrong, but ...?"

Observing the style of adept listeners reminds us that talk is not always what it seems: meanings can hide behind the most innocent of messages and need only the creative probe of the listener to make their presence known. A wide-angle take on what all of it might mean will not only improve your ability to discover the speaker's intent (attitude) but also gain you followers.

Listening's Two Dimensions

In this and the previous chapter, we have seen that listening has a dual reality: think time and response time. Occasionally, the two qualities merge. But the distinct exchanges of comment and rejoinder, or question and answer, are so seldom that they leap out when they do occur. In conversational terms, eyes, face, hands, and body show that we are visually attentive. Verbal responding and feeding back indicate that we are audibly paying attention.

Some people seem naturally more reactive. Others may feel that they will embarrass themselves in front of others if they ask questions or make comments. In his weekly column "On Language" in the Sunday *New York Times Magazine*, columnist William Safire once used an apt analogy that applies equally to the unresponsive listener: "...is like a verb without an object: pale, flat and intransitive."

By contrast, it is said that the tolling of a perfectly made bell creates a corresponding vibration inside the chest of each listener. It is this resonance (or echo)—*and its acknowledgment*—that separates the listening leader from the others.

Connecting with the Listener

Although listeners can do much to establish links with speakers, speakers can also do a great deal to forge bonds with listeners. Each side can help the other make the connection and keep it. And both sides need this help. Communication is, in fact, a two-way street and a complementary process.

The last thing we want to do is talk to ourselves with one or more others present. But how can we talk so people will listen? This is a large subject deserving of lengthier, separate treatment, but the reader should find the following specific guidelines helpful.

Whether you are talking to one other person, a small group, or a large gathering, the goal is the same: effective communication. Like someone who wants to be a good conversationalist. Like the manager or supervisor who wants to conduct a good meeting. Or like the salesperson who has a product, service, or idea to sell. Perhaps you are a teacher, parent, or trainer who has some information or lesson to impart. Or a person who wants to launch a new career or advance a present one. Maybe you aspire to elected office. Or you are a spokesperson representing a company, division, or organization to different publics. In these and other communication situations, speakers tend to think and worry more about what they want to say, rather than making saying it worthwhile. And so they often overlook simple ways to make talk concise, clear, interesting, and engaging.

A Checklist for Facilitating Listening

Here are twelve tips to get others to listen when you talk:

1. *Qualify your listeners.* Think first. Initially consider this question: What kind of mental space do your listeners inhabit? Often there is a serious mismatch between what we want to say and the needs and expectations of listeners. The more we consider their interests and values, the more likely we are to succeed in winning their attention, acceptance, and trust.
2. *Spell out what they can gain.* Never mind that others may know what the topic is. Spell out early what listener(s) will take away from you (a new idea, technique, or opportunity; or clarification of an issue). Make clear why it will be a fair use of their time. This will motivate them to pay closer attention.
3. *Begin on a strong note.* Getting started can be tough. You might open with a rhetorical question—one that doesn't expect an answer (e.g., "What first comes to mind when you hear the word *downsizing*?")—or a headline (e.g.,"The hard facts about software") to command immediate attention. And, if necessary, rehearse the first few lines for smooth, effective delivery. This should help you and others warm up faster.
4. *Provide coming attractions.* Preview your overall remarks. This shows empathy and indicates that you value your listeners' time. Previewing foreshadows what is to come, how time will be spent together. It gives direction and momentum to your words, and provides a help-ful verbal outline.
5. *Draw listeners in.* Others wish to sense that you are with them. Too many speakers remain curiously estranged from their listeners. In-volve others by liberally peppering your talk with inclusive words such as *you*, *your*, and *let's*, along with the usual *I* and *me*. This occasional shift in your focus of attention reduces stress on you while binding you to your audience. In this way, talk becomes a joint venture, not a solo performance.
6. *Keep it "new."* Sometimes, we are at a loss to find ways to keep our remarks fresh. We slacken in our enthusiasm for the subject,

especially if we have talked about it many times before. (It is estimated that one out of five workers suffers from burnout). Use a little
creativity in giving your words fresh appeal. Every day we see much
and hear much yet we use little. Try to venture beyond the bounds
of your conventional thinking. You can draw inspiration from
unexpected sources—from material you may need to read or listen
to in any case. For example, commercial advertising—both print and
radio/television—affords some good examples of analogy, rhetorical
questions, and innovative wordings. With a little focus, observation,
and application, you can adapt these to your own subject. These
inventive touches will help sharpen your ability to continually rediscover your subject. By combining the unlikely in unexpected
ways, you can rev up your creativity engines. This practice will, in
turn, help your listeners know more quickly what you are driving at,
while keeping your own interest level high.

7. *Create realistic moments for rehearsal and practice.* Practicing anything is hardly what most of us would consider a favorite activity.
   And besides, when can you squeeze anything more into an already
   overloaded day? In a world that runs ever faster and in which
   change seems never to be on hold, is it not visionary to expect to
   find any time for practice? Well, that depends on what you mean
   by practice. Waiting until the next conversation, meeting, or presentation makes for slow progress. You can speed up improvement
   by taking advantage of precious tidbits of time (e.g., occasions of
   social conversation or the few moments you may be sitting alone in
   your office or home). Run yourself briefly through three brief steps:
   mouth, move, and *manipulate.* Start by speaking out loud your first
   few lines. Listen to how it sounds in your own ears and then take a
   few moments—sitting or standing—to gesture for the practice of it.
   Get the feel and look of it. Check out your appearance in a mirror.
   Finally, give yourself hands-on practice—literally—with whatever
   form of visual you may plan to use. Just about three to four minutes spent doing this from time to time will do wonders for your
   confidence and delivery. But bear in mind that complacency is self-
   betterment's worst enemy and anxiety its dear friend. It's not a time
   issue; it's a matter of desire.

8. *Disarm your audience.* Speakers don't have to be locked into a formal,
   lecture-type style of speaking. Being more spontaneous is fun, and
   your listeners will appreciate the less formal tone. You can do this by
   commenting now and again on your own remarks or the present

situation. This not only tends to be disarming (listeners don't expect it) but also makes you seem more believable. For example, you might say, "Not a pleasant thought, is it?" Or, "You've heard that many times before, I know." Or, "Sounds hard, doesn't it?" In each case, your stepping out of role (as speaker) provides a welcome commentary and is also a form of empathy.

9. *Exercise quality control.* Ideas don't export easily—they need a delivery system. Motivate listeners by using *contrasting stress accent*, for emphasis; *varied voice inflection*, for interest arousal; *pause,* for impact, listener absorption time, and monitoring listener reaction (and, as we saw earlier, giving listeners a chance to get a word in); *gestures*, for clarity and credibility; *eye orientation*, for conviction; and *facial expression* and *posture*, for animation. These resources, or tools, frame content so that it registers with listeners. The ways we plan our words and engineer our sentences make the difference between a monologue and direct communication with others.

10. *Display your information.* Visualized information has longer staying power (seeing is remembering). But avoid information overload. And develop a sense of timing: conceal until you are ready to reveal (it is all too easy to divide one's attention). Also help listeners maintain focus by sorting out the show and tell, making sure that what you are showing can, in fact, be seen. Clear, uncluttered visuals are best. When talking to a group, position yourself for more profitable speaking by standing to the side of your display.

11. *Handle questions.* In fielding questions, the speaker changes role, and becomes the listener for the moment. Think before answering. Acknowledge the query: for example, it may be a fair, natural, good, tough, or standard question. Summarize or restate the question to prove you're listening and desire to understand, assure that you have accurately understood both the question and its intent, and confirm that both of you are on the same track. By repeating the question before a larger group, you can make sure everyone has heard it, and it buys you a little time to think. At times, you may simply not know the answer (but you will be sure to find out at once, and report right back). Finally, share the answer visually with others present to increase your sphere of influence (another good use of eye contact).

12. *Leave a good impression.* We may think that our message is clear to others. Realistically, it may or may not be. Although our words may be of interest to us, they may not be for our listeners. So, try to talk

in such a way as to help others perceive *value* in your message for themselves. By relating it, in some way, to their experience or responsibilities, there is a better chance of creating productive dialogue, rather than irrelevant one-sided talk.

Achieving Effective Engagement in Conversation

Once learned and practiced, these principles provide a deft game plan that triggers a new sense of confidence and connection. And others are more inclined to listen to you and take you seriously.

Listeners and speakers each have an essential role to play in constructing the bridge that connects them. Reaching out to another removes the unease in the relationship and brings both sides closer together. It is in this act of communion that the viability of a conversation—its very fabric—becomes stronger and more enduring. When all parties do their full share to sustain the relationship, the result can be something greater than the totality: it can, in fact, be a *synergy*.

In summary, when responsiveness is reinstated as a major activity of listeners, and inclusiveness and heightened appeal are cherished values of speakers—both are working to span the communicational divide. And talking time, overall, becomes more productive for everyone.

PART 3

Keeping More of What You Take In

CHAPTER 7

Eleven Tips for Boosting Memory and Recall Ability

Improving your ability to take in information and increasing your level of responsiveness are surely essential to successful listening. But if you are going to profit fully from your key encounters with others, something more is needed. It's not just taking information in that counts; as with earnings, the trick is to hold on to it.

Memory is perishable. Information these days seems to have such a short, fast-moving shelf life. Yet, you must be able to hold on longer to what you take in and be able to bring it to mind when needed.

How can we boost memory? What can we do to keep information from fading? How can we retain—and regain—our hold on information?

Why Does Information Fade So Quickly?

In general, we don't remember things others say because we're too absorbed in our own interests. For example, you know the universal complaint about memory: "When it comes to names, I'm terrible." What keeps so many of us from retaining custody of new names once we've heard them? Often, when introduced to another—either face-to-face or over the phone—we're not really focusing on the other person. We may hear the name, but it doesn't register. Then we feel too embarrassed to ask again. And if we have mentally processed the name, few of us use it right away. So it vanishes from our mind. Left to itself, this negative approach becomes a self-fulfilling prophecy. We almost don't expect that there can be any improvement or control in this area. Sometimes, there are even days when we may think our mind is Teflon coated: nothing sticks!

But there is hope. We can do certain things to increase the chances of remembering and recalling important information—names, dates, numbers, concepts. It doesn't have to be *hear* today, *gone* tomorrow. But things will linger longer when we are more disciplined and apply several techniques *in combination*.

Prolonging the Longevity of Learned Information

1. *Better listening.* Better retention and retrieval begin with better listening in the first place. How much of the time, when we're supposed to be listening, are we self-absorbed and inward-directed? Were we to be honest, we would have to admit that too often we appear narcissistic and withdrawn. Is it any wonder then that information orally communicated to us hardly registers. Our listening goes in and out of focus. We are preoccupied much of the time with our own thoughts and feelings, our own *internal conversation*. It's like trying to take a photo with a lens cap half on: we get a partial image, an over- or underexposed negative. How can we expect then to reconstruct the original?

   As we have seen, when listening becomes *articulate*, focus is sharper, ideas are more vivid and clear, and our listening shows. All of this provides better understanding, a deeper imprint, and a stronger basis for recall. But if one's understanding exceeds one's actions, it won't endure.

2. *Visualization.* Visualization will help you recollect something once heard. Using some form of mental imaging technique can help you make an association between a name, date, or idea and a picture. For example, someone's age is seventy-six. You may associate this fact with a mental picture of the Declaration of Independence (1776). Or, as we learn to do word processing, we come to "see" the various letter keys without looking. It's almost like reading off a mental picture of the keyboard. Then, with more practice, muscle memory takes over and achieves an automatic fluency. Try associating an important fact you wish to remember with an image of some sort in your mind.

   Once on a flight to Boston, I exchanged a few words with a woman seated next to me who worked for a telecommunications company in Atlanta. As the conversation turned to listening, she asked, "You know how I think of listening?" She began to refer to a plastic model of the human brain, with oil poured over the top. She then described how this liquid's movement down through the brain's fissures and crevices reminded her of listening. (I must confess that my first impression was that this was weird. But, over time, I've come to see this as a possible image to call to mind the listening process.)

Visualizing is a form of information imaging. One useful type of visualizing is analogy, a parallel or similar form that gives something new a shape by comparing it to something familiar: for example, thinking of star events as the small meteors hitting the moon, causing impact flashes (brief flashes of light); or, thinking of conversational coordination as the dramatic interplay between orchestra and soloist.

How about feedback as a personal firewall to prevent the intrusion of distraction? Or perhaps you may have seen the political cartoon of former president Bill Clinton trying to make a diving catch of a large ball: the ball, labeled "greatness," lands just out of his reach. The mind tends to retain these visual metaphors more easily than text (a picture is worth how many words?).

I came across one image I especially like while perusing the science section of a major daily newspaper. Reading about the so-called noble gases—those standoffish chemical elements that resist pairing up with other atoms (e.g., helium, neon)—made me think of unreactive listeners. Interestingly, the report mentions that argon recently lost its "hermit (inert no more) status."

As with most things, this kind of exercise becomes easier the more you do it. You might inquire of friends and coworkers what mental pictures they conjure up to remember their various important facts.

3. *Write it down.* Sure it sounds simple, but many people still feel they can ignore this easy way of retaining information. Or they may feel squeamish and suffer from a kind of intrusion sensitivity. They mistakenly think that the other person will mind their taking a few notes or even writing one or two words down on paper. Ever since the introduction of writing to human civilization, making marks on a surface has obviously helped information to persist.

Let's face it, in just about every case, the issue of recalling vital information—people's names, sales data, directions, instructions— is much more important than one's feelings of inadequacy. So, re- member to give yourself this obvious advantage. And, if you abso- lutely must, ask the person you're conversing with whether he or she minds your taking some notes. Invariably, people won't mind. And they'll be flattered by your added measure of interest in what they're saying. Keep in mind, too, that perhaps more today than at any other time in history, we are severely weighed down by information overload. Data transferred to paper, CD, or laptop computer make the load more manageable.

4. *Try relating the information to yourself.* Studies show that this is another effective way of keeping important information fresh and accessible. Yet don't be too literal about this: it could be to refer something to immediate or extended family or to your neighbors. Someone's birth date may be the same as yours, or it may fall in your month or week. A color requested by a customer may be your favorite one. This association strengthens the stimulation and enhances the chances of recall. This is a helpful notion when it comes to remembering names. For example, when I am reviewing in preparation for training a new group, I try to think of some family member or neighbor I know who has the same first name as one of the participants. I then make that conscious link.

   In one of my listening workshops, a fellow said to me: "If you can help me remember the name of one of my best friends, I'll think that the day will have been worth it." When I asked him the name of his friend, he said: "Secor." I immediately replied, "It sounds like Seymour." Expressing both delight and amazement, he then confessed, "I've never thought of that!" We can consciously forge associations of various kinds and thus tilt the chances of better recall in our favor.

5. *Review.* Be sure to review on a regular basis what you need to remember. This *repetitive retrieval* forces facts to the forefront of your mind, keeping them fresh and available. Depending on their importance and timeliness, you may want to use this technique frequently throughout the day or week. It's much like retracing the outline of a faded diagram or providing a fresh coat of paint to a dry, weather-worn fence (there are two more visual metaphors for you).

6. *Alliteration.* As another useful memory aid, alliteration is stringing together two or more words beginning with the same first sound or letter: for example, *fiscal philosophy, walking the wrong way, conscious convergence* (remember?), *deep discounts, monstrous machines, the healing power of hobbies,* or—and this creative example appeared as the title of a recent newspaper article—*tourist tips tailored to teenagers.* By noting—and even creating—the doubling (or tripling) of the first sound or letter, you are making these events more prominent in your mind and therefore more memorable. Think of this as an encoding device.

7. *Rhyming.* As another encoding device, rhyming works much the same way. Few of us will forget the old adage: April showers bring May flowers, or Thirty days hath September, April, June, and November. And, as you may remember, one of the many contemporary aspirin-like medicines has promoted itself with the words "All day strong. All day long." This is yet another way to raise something heard out of the ordinary mass of sounds.

8. *Mnemonics.* Then of course there is the age-old memory device, the mnemonic. These are today's acronyms, of which there seems to be an almost infinite number: from long-established ones such as IRS, GM, and NBC to more recently coined abbreviations such as DSL (digital subscriber line), SUV (sport utility vehicle), and IM (instant messaging). There are so many encapsulated reminders that, to the initiated, quickly summon to mind the constituent elements for which they stand. Try using your own creativity to make up some of your own for practical purposes.

   Acronyms put information in compressed form, which can then be pressed into service in short order, as needed. They are a kind of shorthand that makes its way more easily into and out of an already overcrowded mind.

9. *Reiteration.* Few of us take advantage of saying something over to another. This is productive repetition. While working out at a local gym, I met an acquaintance who was on the medical faculty of a university hospital. He suggested the name of a colleague he thought I should contact in connection with a communications project I was working on. Not having pen and paper to jot it down, I focused hard on the first and last name of this individual. Then, jumping into the pool, I kept repeating his name over and over as I swam my laps. (This was, I will admit, pushing the idea of being "resourceful" a bit far, but I was determined to keep this valuable bit of information from slipping my mind.) When I came out, I said it out loud a few times. When I arrived at my office, it was still fresh in my mind, and I was able to write it down on a piece of paper.

   More generally, try to find reasons for bringing up in conversation some new information you have acquired. It might be a name, an idea, an issue, or a concern—something you want to keep in the forefront of your mind for long-term preservation. You will be surprised at how easily you can slip such new information bits into your daily talk with colleagues, family members, and friends. They probably will not notice anything unusual, and you will be succeeding in keeping such necessary information close at hand.

10. *Thinking outside of the box.* This means occasionally getting beyond the conventional, making a thoughtful foray outside your normal lines of business (and perception). This opens up a whole new world of creative associations (solutions), or analogies. For example, most people know that an electrical storm can destroy your modem if there is no surge protector on the telephone line (preventable by a UPS, uninterruptible power supply). This might suggest the role of listener responsiveness as a surge protector for the mind (that is, an uninterruptible concentration supply). Moving slightly into the vision field, one might speak of star events as creating a kind of focal cataract condition, whereby the mind becomes clouded, impairing perception.

11. *Leisure activities.* Don't overlook the restorative benefits of leisurely activities and exercise: walking, jogging, reading, tennis, drawing or painting, yoga, gardening, swimming, aerobics, playing or listening to music, basketball, dance, writing. These, and other forms of relaxation and bodily movement, provide stimulation and healthful benefits not only for a well-functioning body but also for a clearheaded mind. In my case, I like to swim laps. After every swimming experience, I emerge honestly feeling several years younger; my mind—cleared of the mental "cobwebs"—appears more alert and retentive, and I even seem to be able to think more clearly. Surely any such improvement to respiration and circulation can be expected to enhance mental performance and overall well-being.

A Summary of Practical Pointers

Remember, the mind is a faulty container—there's always some leakage. So how can we improve storage and recall ability?

- Start by resolving to be a better listener in the first place—both in receiving and feeding back.
- Try to visualize in some way what you need to remember.
- Do write it down.
- See if you can relate the information in some way to yourself or others.
- Commit to actively retrieving this information at various intervals.
- Be creative in taking advantage of alliteration.
- Equally, on occasion, try your hand at rhyming.

- Come up with your own acronyms, compressing data into shorthand formulas, for more efficient storage and easier recall.
- Find moments in conversation—with coworkers, friends, and family members—when you can insert or bring up some new name, idea, fact, or issue that you want to keep fresh in your mind.
- Once in a while, mentally wander outside your circumscribed, everyday world, and let your ears and eyes take in something new (a word or phrase, image, or concept) that might give you a different and fresh perspective on something you wanted to remember.
- And don't forget: another reason to relax or exercise your body regularly is to give your mind a welcome tune-up.

In combination, these tips can give a powerful boost to your memory and instant recall ability.

CHAPTER 8

Three Ways to Keep Listening Sharp

Your improved new ability to listen needs safeguards to maintain its peak performance. Without them, you will revert to old habits and tendencies. The remedy is not a quick read of a book but finding ways to renew amid our everyday experiences. How do you keep something alive? With a living organism—a human being, animal, or plant—you caringly provide food and nutriment. With an inanimate product of mind and life experience— an idea, belief, skill, or technique—you might think about it, talk or write about it, teach it to others, possibly express it as an art form, certainly practice and use it.

The critical threshold of pain for most training programs and individual self-improvement efforts is whether mastery of the skills is worth the effort. We can cross that threshold by defining more value and providing strong motivation, as I have tried to do in this book. But there is a little skepticism in all of us. Anyone who has ever lived has dreamed; anyone who has struggled to change has memories of disappointment as well as occasional triumph. Listeners are no exception.

Avoiding the Trap of Disillusionment

Many people experience a high after reading a self-help book. They may experience a rush of adrenaline and perhaps feel, for a limited time, inspired to recommit themselves to applying some of the lessons they have learned. They may even have a sense of new beginnings. But all too often, this new readiness to do loses steam, and our game plan is put on a burner too far back. (It is a disturbing fact that the world is full of well-intentioned folks who have stopped too soon or may never have started.)

Faced by the everyday pressures of work, travel, family and more, it's easy to become disillusioned. When things change—and ours is a quick-change world—motivation and confidence are often lost. But they don't have to be; they can grow. Skills we have learned or enlarged can remain fresh and relevant. But we need to attack the problem in a realistic and constructive way. In earlier chapters, we reviewed some of the critical background to listening and specific ways to manage this skill more efficiently and effectively to enhance mutual understanding and respect. This has raised our awareness. Yet to control this ability, we must nurture and keep this awareness.

There's a great gap, after all, between understanding something and doing it. Containment tools and convergence techniques give us directions and signposts along the road to better listening. But how can we internalize them? How can we increase their long-lasting holding power and our own ease of execution? The answer lies in incorporating these skills within our own personal styles and making them our own.

The Powerful Actions-Attitudes Principle

It has been said that success is a choice. It is also true that people have possibilities that have never been realized. We need to rededicate ourselves. A higher level of resolve is necessary, yet we also need something more.

What, you may well ask, another motivational spiel? Not really. On the contrary, there is something you may not have thought of that actually works. It is deceptively simple, but has enormous potency: *the actions-attitudes principle*. Put simply, we are molded by our own actions. Actions draw feelings. Actions shape attitudes. Or, as the world-renowned developmental psychologist Jerome Bruner put it more powerfully (as quoted in a training newsletter): "We are more likely to act ourselves into feeling than feel ourselves into acting." Attitudes and feelings are as much formed by, as lead to, concrete actions (good practices).

While watching the televised tennis match between Gabriella Sabatini and Lindsay Davenport, I unexpectedly experienced this truth. Each player seemed to display equal assurance and skill in returning the other's volley. During one particularly thrilling series of back-and-forth exchanges,

Davenport's hard return of the ball caught just enough of the upper taped portion of the net to bounce back into her half of the court. As the crowd moaned its disappointment—tinged with empathy for the player—one saw her suddenly become visibly agitated and upset. I vividly remember the announcer (Billie Jean King) broadcasting over the airwaves to a national audience: "She shouldn't get down on herself like that. I know how she feels," adding something about how, even though she's upset, she should still put on a positive demeanor. And then the words: "Because the mind begins to imitate the body."

Such overt, physical behaviors (standing erect, a smile on the face, one hand's fist punching the palm of the other) are not external effects artificially grafted on, but a continuing, deeply integral part of who or what we are. This quite simply means that every time you perform some act, you affect not only another's perception of you but also your own perception of yourself. A familiar example of this is the way we shake hands with someone (culturally defined, in part). I won't debate with you whether it is right or wrong, but parts of our society place a negative value on a weak, or limp, handshake. By shaking someone's hand more firmly, not only do we create a more positive perception in the other person but also, at the same time, we change the way we think and feel *about ourselves*.

There is a powerful message here. Even though our hearts may not have arrived as yet, it is still important to use our lips to communicate the commitment. As they say, you start by talking the talk; you will eventually come to walk the walk. This is not theory; it is fact. It may sound far-fetched to some readers, but it is actually accurate. And you have already demonstrated this numerous times in your various life accomplishments, even though you are probably unaware of it.

Now let's apply this understanding to improving listening performance and maintaining peak performance over the long term. If we are really serious about this, we should act accordingly. We will then feel the impact and reinforcement of our actions. Once we attain this mind set, our positive actions will transform our thoughts and feelings. This can be accomplished in three ways: doing, observing, and visualizing.

Doing

How do you think good performers—sports figures, musicians, artists, writers—come by their mastery? That's right, through practice. It's the same with listening. In fact, great listeners never stop practicing because they recognize that this ability needs constant nurturing. We come to know something by *doing* it (music, by playing it; a subject, by teaching it; listening, by practicing it).

As with any skilled performance, you can obviously practice good listening technique by listening; for example, consciously ask open-ended questions, or deliberately try to restate out loud what you think you have heard. In this way, you are challenging yourself to gain fluency, facility, and ease of execution in the language of listening.

But you get an even bigger payoff: Every time you make a deliberate effort—a conscious convergence—to connect with your conversational partner, you boost your self-confidence at the same time.

Observing

Good practices are not only taught but also "caught"—by *observing* good role models. But observation is not only a matter of vision; it requires training and the willingness to notice pattern and detail.

To achieve sustainable new growth, we need to proceed slowly and systematically. Sharp-eyed observation of listening performance can also materially affect our attitude and execution. With the proliferation of meetings, conference-calls, and training seminars today, managers and supervisors have many more opportunities to model exemplary communicators and how they perform in the listener role.

A newly appointed project manager once told me, "I tend to tune meetings out." This unfortunate attitude means lost opportunities for him. Granted, most organizations hold too many meetings, and all too few are truly stimulating and productive. Nevertheless, we have seen that being an opportunist and tuning in, now and then, can help you catch someone doing something good (a helpful reminder) or something bad (another kind of reminder).

Once I stopped to watch the butcher in the supermarket cutting off strips of fat from some pieces of meat. As I looked on with interest, he suddenly looked up and said, "Good morning." Smiling, I replied, "Good morning. I was watching your technique." He said, "When I'm off the job for a while or so (on vacation), and come back, my cutting is off." He then added, "You have to do it all the time." So it is with developing facility in any skill. *You have to do it all the time.*

Remember, amid some dross, there can be a vein of gold. Vigilant eyes and ears can pick up a lot. When looking at television, watch the interplay between talk show hosts and their guests, or newscasters commenting on the news. Observe how others use verbal strategies such as restatement or acknowledgment as nonconfrontational, yet persuasive ways to let the speaker know what the listeners are thinking and feeling. For example, you can easily expand your own "response-arsenal" (listening vocabulary) by adapting apt phrases you may overhear others using.

Similarly, noticing also how accomplished listeners cope with emotional turbulence suggests that such events need not upend a determined effort to maintain equilibrium, but responsive work will be required. Observing a great listener can also be a lesson in how to blend the private and the public dimensions of listening. Others can be role models for us, either positive or negative, allowing us to reframe our realities and salvage more value from situations we are in.

Of course, if you can use your company's video equipment to record and observe yourself in a simulated conversation, so much the better. This contributes a strong motivational factor. When you see it, it has a personal impact.

Visualizing

Another way that accomplished performers keep their edge is through *visualization*. For example, the best golfers are known to fully visualize their swing before they hit the ball. The most effective teachers visualize their lesson presentations before they deliver them. Through self-guided imagery, you see yourself performing the task in question as your mind moves through the various steps involved. Similarly, by engaging in this mental dress rehearsal, a listener enters a conversation in a higher state of preparedness.

To be more precise, we should speak of audiovisualization, because we give off audible as well as visible signs when we listen effectively. So, for instance, you can hear yourself (in your mind's ear) validating another's expressed emotion or reflecting the underlying implication in what you heard. As a result, you will arrive on the scene already warmed up and more confident than you would be otherwise.

The Payoff of Persistence

I like to think of listening performance as a language of conduct in which we want to be fluent and flexible. ("Oh, no," I hear some of you saying. "I was never good at languages." Don't lose heart. It's not what you think. Besides, it can be much *less* time-consuming and arduous than what you remember in the classroom.) Practice to attain these attributes. Hold loftier expectations of yourself. Quality doesn't have to take a long time. Stick with a personal game plan you can live with. Practice something, in some way, every day. Your successes will begin to bolster you.

Don't be discouraged by an off moment, an off day, or a conversation that did not go well. Everyone has them. They are but temporary set-backs. Just continue your program. As they say in sales: "There is no such thing as a loser, only someone who has stopped too soon." Don't be too hard on yourself, but do persevere.

You will come to feel empowered by a new attitude. In the early stages, your responsiveness may be handled with reasonable precision, but so programmed are the formulated phrases that one could picture the promptings in the text. This is normal. In time you will listen with a more relaxed manner as listening gradually comes without any sense of forcing. Calculated, conscious responses will yield to spontaneous ones, becom-ing a natural and unself-conscious process. Realize that you don't have to be anyone's clone; you can put your personal stamp on these techniques and carve your own identity. And in so doing, you will take a professional turn for the better. Practice gives you the feeling of being one up on everyone else.

The Creative Capacity for Renewal

Doing. Observing. Audiovisualizing. With these three techniques, the essence of renewal is captured. And you keep your listening from going stale. Seek out opportunities to exercise your listening abilities in one or all of these ways. You may be overdoing it a bit at first. Don't worry. As you move in this positive direction, you will soon find the right balance. As you master the lessons of articulate listening, you will gradually de-velop a voice and vision of your own. Remember, more realistic than "practice makes perfect" (we don't have to be perfect) is *practice makes permanent* (the famous words, I believe, of legendary football coach Vince Lombardi): the more you do, the more the skills will remain with you, and the more adept you will become.

PART 4

The Listening Leader—Revisited

CHAPTER 9

Listening and Leadership

Today, some would say that we are blessed with a burgeoning number and variety of electronic devices that are shrinking our world and keeping us all connected. Yet, ironically, even as the world becomes smaller, there is a growing sense of interpersonal distance. And our ever busier, speeded-up lives make us painfully aware of the increasing strain to which listening is put.

Traditionally, listening has embraced the individual's private life. Relationship was not an item on the intellectual agenda in the last century. So listeners have viewed conversation as less ensemble and more solo voiced. Yet one cannot confine listening within the space allocated by society to reception and understanding without robbing it of its breadth, richness, and influence. Managers and supervisors are stymied by a lack of real connection with direct reports. Employees are inhibited by a sense of distrust. Salespeople feel emotionally removed from buyers. And customers, unengaged by salespeople, view them with suspicion or disdain. The compartmentalized identity is out of step with the corporate reality of business life.

Listening in the New Millennium

As we continue in the twenty-first century, listening will become a more critical—and valued—skill. The key to more effective, efficient organizations, after all, is the improved quality of conversations and relationships.

And a crucial component of success is *the ability to listen in the widest sense*. As team management, consultative selling, and leadership development become more pressing business priorities, the notion of listening will also acquire a broader, more flexible definition. Today—and tomorrow—greater success will come from more fully realized listener–speaker collaboration as well.

To connect more deeply with others for mutual success today, we must develop a very different perception of what it is to be a listener. To paraphrase John F. Kennedy's speech given at Amherst College, MA, on October 26, 1963, in praise of the poet, Robert Frost, on the nature of art: *If listening is to fulfill its true mission, society must set the listener free to connect. We must never forget that listening is not a form of solitude, it is a form of engagement.* The very feeling of marginality must give way to conversational relatedness if this perception is to be the content and basis of a new mode of listening. Indeed, a new set of attitudes has emerged in the last two decades, sharply at odds with the assumptions that had governed most of listening in the past century. And in the early twenty-first century, these perceptions have acquired a new urgency and relevance.

It's not just about having unsurpassed control of concentration. It's about getting others to share information easily—and openly—with people they can trust. Besides verbal competence, one needs listening aptitude and sensitivity to achieve productive human encounters in meetings, interviews, and negotiations—dialogue conducted artfully from the palette of such basic elements as questions, restatement, acknowledgment, facial expression, and emotional validation.

The contemporary listener needs to move things along at a snappier pace; to understand others more deeply and accurately; to achieve an easier, closer rapport; and to forge stronger bonds. Our listening must be more demonstrative—to disclose its presence and reflect the speaker's state of mind with bodily attitudes, gestures, facial expressions, movements of the eyes, and verbal feedback.

True leaders are expressive listeners. By renewing powers we have forfeited, and accommodating to a more interactive listening style, we can also create a more powerful influence capable of shaping both a conversation's goals and its outcomes.

Those who would influence others exemplify the qualities of *articulate listening*. They recognize that attending closely to what others are saying—and facilitating their ability to be more forthcoming and honest in their communications—is an extension of their own leadership.

Increasingly, listening dispatched with discipline and quality control will yield greater reward in terms of interpersonal balance of power, equalizing the relationship, conversational productivity, influence, and personal meaning.

Balance of Power

Participants in conversation have the possibility of remaining separate or moving forward together to form a cohesive unit. Listening is a matter of choice.

But we normally assume that the speaker–listener relationship is one in which all the deference is on the listener's side and all the power is on the speaker's side. We have seen the usual scenario: While the speaker goes on talking, the listener keeps casual, silent stride, seemingly not overly interested. Connections are few, responding is repressed, and the mood lethargic. The minimal response even seems superficial, as though nothing more is required, and so we remain only distantly involved. It is almost as if we are present at some event (like passively watching television). The performance lacks nuance in matters of questioning, nonverbal expression, and responding. *The narrow model of the 'ideal' listener has grown deep roots.*

Typically, too many managers still operate within this limiting, traditional framework.

Equalizing the Relationship

The articulate listening style changes the terms of engagement. Enhancing the listener's power-projection capabilities—through response and feedback—it suggests that the scales can be pretty well balanced. Today, as listeners discover the language of connection, the relational landscape of business conversation is beginning to change. Speakers are no longer the *sole* influencers. No more are they the only ones who impact, define, and steer the conversation. And the secondary position that convention has accorded the listener is giving way to one more resembling a side-by-side status with the speaker.

The speaker–listener relationship is one of several traditional reciprocals—others including doctor–patient, manager–associate, teacher–student, and parent–child—in which power is typically vested in the first member. This new power-sharing arrangement transcends the traditional conversational hierarchy that placed listeners in a subordinate, secondary role to power-wielding, influence-exercising talkers. To be sure, listeners have some catching up to do in this regard. But as our perception of the listener's identity and role in conversation changes, and we cast ourselves in this new, more prominent light, influence will shift more and more to the listening side. And a long-accumulated legacy of self-doubt and stigma can be lifted.

As an interactive, articulate listener, we have the potential to level the interpersonal playing field so that dialogue can be more efficient and results oriented. Articulate listening is a listening practiced toward the speaker. And its style is more in keeping with contemporary desires. In a 2004 employee survey conducted by the Mulvaney Group, a New York based consulting organization dealing with diversity and workforce development programs, 60 percent of respondents said they would like to change corporate cultures to be more inclusive. The same may be said of conversations. Now there can be deeper connections where there had been dissociation. The new perception supplies listener identity with a content and direction. It is feedback, after all, that gives the listener a recognizable public profile. Response and feedback, as we have seen, can indeed offer access to power. (It is tempting to find a parallel with the political candidate who has found an issue to embrace.)

As listeners becoming leaders assume a larger ownership stake in conversation, they will become major players with the speaker (partners in power). By expanding range, versatility, and sensitivity of responding, managers, salespeople, and others will enhance their status as leaders and set a new tone for all parties to succeed as equals.

It is time for listeners to break the mold of conventional thought. To do this, they must know how to tame the demons of distraction, distortion, and defensiveness that have traditionally driven listening, and find their voice. Teams, departments, and companies will grow and prosper when they abandon listening practices that for decades have undermined trust and squandered time and opportunities.

It will take vision, organizational commitment, and individual persistence, but in terms of the practical consequences of greater commitment and cooperation, the results will greatly repay the effort. Listening is at its strongest and most penetrating when it engages the speaker. And, in these terms, listening can be tapped as a new power source for conversational systems.

Productivity

Companies have to be more customer oriented today. But this is not just a matter of providing precise software (or other product) solutions to ensure the customers' success. Services, too, are increasingly important (the U.S. economy's service sector continues to grow exponentially). *You're not a leader unless you make things happen, unless you deliver results.* And this applies as much to quality of service as it does to delivering goods and meeting production quotas or sales goals. In particular, this must include listening—being more responsive—to the buyer. And when listening is articulate, there is the ability to establish rapport quickly, communicate ideas efficiently, and bring minds together. Whether in face-to-face or tele-conferencing meetings, interviews, and conversations, the listening leader can substantially improve the gains in communication and results.

A company's productivity and industry leadership is slowed when listeners act like clogged fuel injectors: slow, sluggish, unresponsive. We can take a lesson from skilled speakers: they have more stage presence—and influence—than average or mediocre speakers precisely because their speaking is so much a matter of *action*. So it also is for the few rare listening leaders.

Observe them in their listening relationships. The quality is distinctive. Exceptional attention is the first impression. The mainstream listener diffuses his concentration energies. The listening leader is different in that he or she maintains superb concentration and focus, and listens with deliberate intent. The traditional listener is fixated on him or herself. The listening leader centers attention on the speaker and keeps the urge to take over the talking in tow.

This aptly describes one aspect of the articulate listening style—*containment* (controlled concentration)—marked by a conspicuous lack of struggle and self-absorption. There is clear demonstration of continued listening against tough odds. The average listener is often unready to listen and frequently checks out of the conversation. The leader comes prepared to listen, checks in early, and remains securely connected to the speaker and the message.

But attention is not all that the listener has to give. The distinctive qualities of an articulate listener—liveliness, sophistication, and an abiding concern for others—are apparent in the frequency and manner of *converging with the speaker*. As leaders, these listeners commit themselves wholeheartedly to the challenge of conversation and take great pride in the effort. Standard listeners seem uninvolved and devoid of interest. Listening leaders seem fully engaged. Their listening reflects personal involvement and excitement with the message as well as commitment to the speaker's meaning. And they deeply respect the continuity of a conversation. They are fellow travelers in the conversation, and their partners keenly feel their engagement.

And, in significant and timely fashion, we find this reflected in a paraphrase here of a *New York Times* editorial at New Year 2000: Beneath these flurries of corporate consolidation and middle-class materialism, more humanistic aspirations are quickening as well—a yearning for a conversational encounter that is as engaging as it is productive.

In short, these listeners meet a speaker's expectations by demonstrating their shared conviction that a message is not something to passively listen to or merely enjoy but to ponder, study, respond to, learn about, and ask questions about. Acting in the speaker's best interest, the listening leader offers a listening style that has presence, character, and connection.

The choice has widened significantly. And thus understood, articulate listening is a policy of greater involvement. These listeners' obvious commitment to the speaker, and their practiced execution, make emotionally secure, relationally attuned listening leaders a possible dream.

Leadership listening is the key to more effective and productive meetings and negotiations. The proceedings are marked by fewer contentions and divisive issues, reduced downtime, and increased efficiency.

Listening leaders also have an immediate, positive impact on the performance level of teams. Their fluid, quick-responding, conversation-sharing style readily builds motivation and trust. Team members feel the leader's palpable presence. And instead of tracing divergent paths, there is a convergence of thought and feeling among all present. They find themselves not only on the same page but *in the same paragraph*.

Just as most employers prefer in their people the qualities of determination, good judgment, and self-discipline, much the same may be said of listening. No matter what type of work you do, the way you listen can *differentiate* you from others (in a good sense) and even provide an extra measure of job security. Your ability to fully listen in key areas—interviews (media, job, or sales), presentations, performance appraisals, trade shows, conferences, and meetings—shows you to be a superior professional worth keeping in hard times and worth promoting when times are better.

And let's not forget one more thing. Just as important for the corporate conversations of the future are the declining business costs of more efficient and effective engagements. Organizations must look to the outcomes of not only their projects but also their discussions. Team members should feel that they could get their manager's or supervisor's attention when they need it. Buyers must perceive that a salesperson cares not only about the sale but also about *them*.

And here, too, the listening leader contributes mightily. He or she knows that conversations come to life in the exchanges and interactions of all parties. The listener understands that they are quickened by fresh, clear, well-articulated responses. Speaker and listener alike serve as mutual catalysts fueling each other's performance. And these listeners don't let distraction cloud the message. Rather, they work to create an atmosphere in which everyone concerned seems to be working within a shared conception of the conversation, mentally and emotionally. We might say, "They recognize that a listener is, or should be, the speaker's projection screen."

Although some of them may not be able to grasp everything accurately the first time, they know this important truth: Listening in these terms is leadership, not just a temporary stop on the way to real communication.

A major investment bank's ad in a leading newspaper stated: "The partnership approach: the closer the understanding, the greater the trust, and the more productive the partnership." The traditional listener has worked out of the spotlight. The listening leader reminds us of how much a listener can accomplish when he or she joins the speaker at center stage.

Influence

Most listeners are unlikely to attach influential significance to feedback. This is partially because it looks suspiciously like an attempt to preempt the speaker and also because they have not thought of listener response in terms of empowerment. For many managers, rebuttal still comes more naturally than restatement, confrontation more readily than reconciliation. Few know how to be supportively—not competitively—present in a conversation. And not many have the ability to manage a speaker's communication (conversational stewardship). Indeed, it almost seems sometimes that *we renounce compromise, or acknowledgment, out of a moral passion to be right.*

"You're not listening to me," she asserted in a strong tone. She was now looking at me defiantly. Her sudden, sharp words resonated in my ears like a metal ball bouncing off metal surfaces. They cut me painfully to the quick. My mind was a muddle of emotions: I felt unjustly accused, unappreciated, disappointed, misunderstood. As pride kept me from seeing and feeling beyond myself, I wanted to tell her she was wrong. But my wife is not one to pull punches with me; she lets me know—flat out— how I'm coming across to her. Yet, I still wanted to rebut, to set aright, to justify, to defend. But was I in touch at all with how *she* was feeling? Had I any notion of why she had felt cheated and emotionally shortchanged in our conversation?

How often, I wonder, is this scene—or one like it—played out in other marriage relationships, selling situations, or peer interactions? Typically, in our daily exchanges, we know where we are going, but often don't take time to figure out where others are coming from. Besides, amid the rush and turmoil in today's workplace, we must often catch someone's words on the fly. It is hard to slow our minds and bodies down—and turn down our own inner radios—long enough to pick up the broadcasts of others. But let's go back to the previous scenario, and put the video on pause for a moment.

Suppose, instead of soothing my ego and defending against my wife's verbal accusation, I had had the presence of mind and willpower to say something like "I'm sorry, hon. I didn't mean to cut you off." Or, "I'm sorry; I should have acknowledged how you felt." True, these words are coming after the fact. But now, she discerns a difference. And, by getting in touch with her feelings, this goodwill gesture could still cause a positive change in her attitude. Better yet, deployed earlier, such a welcome comment could defuse emotional turmoil—on either side of the exchange—before it starts causing problems.

Who suffers when the manager's listening intention is not fulfilled? The conversational partner, obviously. The failed expectations of others give rise to negative perceptions of the manager. But what many managers fail to realize when their listening intention is not fulfilled is that these problems others experience *are also their own.* If direct reports, peers, customers, and bosses can't get a sense of being fully understood and received in conversation, they feel the manager is not listening. Eventually, it's going to be very difficult for the manager to gain—and keep—their cooperation, trust, and loyalty. So managers can blame others, if they must, for not being clear, forthcoming, and honest; but they must also understand that, sooner or later, they are going to have to pay the price of unfulfilled listening intentions.

To be fair, few managers don't listen at all. But the far more serious problem is that few managers discharge their *full* listening responsibilities by using functional feedback to build engagement and meaningful rapport. In fact, less-than-complete listening—a problem that virtually every manager faces—is the fundamental cause of limited sharing, low morale, low confidence, and low productivity. The manager then has to work much harder (and often without success) to get to the root of real issues and concerns. And the team, department, and organization lack the inner cohesive strength to succeed and grow.

Leaders are team players who want to help others succeed. But leaders need followers, and people will only follow someone whom they can trust. Just as consumers are becoming activists—less passive, more participative—so too managers and other would-be leaders must become more outer focused and get on more intimate terms with feedback, if they want people to feel good about their commitment and integrity.

Interest and empathy are strong motivators. And the listening leader uses feedback so that the essential need to receive should be counterbalanced by the senses of being received. A speaker is emboldened by feedback. In fact, the variety and vitality of the feedback creates the kind of style people are more likely to respond to. One of the effects of such a congenial style is to intensify the feeling of identification between the speaker and listener, and between the listener and the speaker's message. And another is to *intensify the speaker's capacity for sharing*. A listener should be an attentive collaborator who helps a speaker successfully express what he or she is trying to communicate.

Leaders are no accidental listeners. They leave nothing to chance, but are quick to take advantage of the tactical wisdom of gestures of acknowledgment and empathy. This is what great listeners do, something more than passively registering incoming data. *They actually create and empower*. And this way, they can influence others not only to listen but to change and work differently as well.

Because commerce and industry are driven by the harsh winds of competition and the economy, every organization has a critical interest in seeing that its people listen up to their capabilities. Today's leading companies care (or should care) about the quality of communication that they provide to their customers. Increasingly, they will seek out—and rely on—listening leaders to deliver the continuous connection and immediate response that today's rapid-fire conversations demand. Their customers can then feel assured in the knowledge that they will receive the attention and concern they need and expect.

The message for aspiring listening leaders is clear: the listening effort is mind-set over matter. And the day is coming when listening will no longer be perceived as a badge of passivity and a source of distraction but as a symbol of communicational leadership and a claim to distinction.

Personal Meaning

Clearly, the value of listener engagement as a communicational ideal is of the highest necessity in our professional lives and for the leaders of our day—executives, managers and supervisors, engineers, scientists, consultants and advisers, salespeople, and others in highly visible and responsible roles. But what does this mean to you personally? What significance, more generally, does the notion of listening leader have for you as an individual? In this section, we will distill from our evolving discussion a *set of realizations*, and briefly consider some implications of the new perception for the contemporary listener's identity, role, and self-image.

Throughout this book, serious and sustained reflection has made us aware of a very different perception of what it is to be a listener today. A helpful and overarching distinction now emerges, which may be phrased as *authenticity* versus *inauthenticity* as a listener. Simply put, the authentic listener is one who fulfills his role as listener, who performs to the fullest his role as listener. Here, we identify the *listening leader* (the professional—e.g., the supervisor or manager—who fulfills his or her listening mandate). The inauthentic listener is one who limits the listening role or tries to escape from it. And here we recognize the *traditional listener*.

Within this framework, a most important realization has to do with freedom. Breaking with the past, listening leaders foster a new sense of freedom—both for themselves and for their speaking partners. *When we tap into the attitude-changing potential of feedback, we can liberate ourselves from preconceived notions and historic trappings.* Listeners will become less reserved, more open-minded. Speakers will be freed from the anxiety of guesswork, no longer wondering if the message was heard, understood, or considered. And they will feel they can express themselves more freely and will do so more aptly. The road of listening becomes a lot smoother. Results come faster and more easily.

Even more so, reaching beyond past limitations offers the listening leader a chance to bravely shape *a new persona*—by fashioning a new voice out of various response options. Containment tools and convergence techniques plug these professionals into the pulse of colleagues and customers. They listen with sensitive understanding, firm up relationships, and increase cooperation and sales. Articulate listening, in essence, gives listeners back their personality. And in responsive feedback, it imbues them with a true humanity that is otherwise missing.

Equally significant, this newfound freedom brings about a fundamental change in the listener's identity, role, and self-image. As long as listeners perceived themselves as no more than peripheral and subordinate to speakers in conversation, theirs was a *vicarious identity*–they were essentially defined by the output of the speaker. But as managers or supervisors begin to think differently as listeners, and come to believe that listening can leverage higher levels of mutual understanding and rapport, they will expand the bounds of their leadership role. And their self-perception will be greatly enhanced: there will be more confidence, more assertiveness, and more openness.

Yet another valuable realization is this: most listeners don't realize that response plays a major role in improving focus. It is a major element in concentration control. All that is reflected back to the speaker—verbal responses, facial expression, body positioning—*is not external to focus, but an intrinsic part of its order.* Response can be a hedge against distraction.

Listening leaders also help us realize something else that is important: In conversational listening, concentration *can* coexist with collaboration, and processing with participation. And they demonstrate this in their commitment to listening, manifest behavior, and thinking. In the process, they maximize their real time in listening and improve the quality of contact in conversations.

And articulate listening, the most fundamental power tool the listening leader has, separates essential details from extraneous ones in a speaker's message. This is somewhat akin to the communication engineer's concern to reduce—or eliminate—background static (noise) in transmission lines. In both cases, we might say that we are working to increase the ratio of signal to noise.

Perhaps most important, we find ourselves forgetting—or don't even realize—the enormous transformational change that our own actions engender in our attitudes and feelings. Make no mistake, the mind *does* imitate the body. And this is the surest way to make steady progress in developing any set of skills: for our purpose, becoming a more socially minded, speaker-affirming listener. As Eric Hoffer once put it, in, I believe, *The True Believer* (Harper & Row, 1951), "Kindness can become its own motive. We are made kind by being kind."

Complete listening brings greater fulfillment and joy to those seeking personal meaning in their personal, family, and professional lives. And these values need restating in a tumultuous world.

We've seen in the twentieth century a nation and a world reshaped by revolutions in communications, transportation, medicine, and commerce. In the twenty-first century, we have the potential—and opportunity—to reinvent ourselves. Few of us will be sorry to see the listener's old persona go: inadequate and dated both in outlook and behavior, it gave the listener little chance to be a full partner with the speaker—as comanager and motivator of the conversation—and to forge that possibility into reality.

It has been suggested that to move toward a better future means to renounce—or rebalance—some aspect of the past. This certainly rings true with respect to the listening enterprise. *It means drawing the line between conversation and listening differently from that established in the last century.* A new perception must come to dominate listener attitudes. And *self-disclosure* should be the watchword of the modern listener who maneuvers through a conversation filled with land mines of distraction and differing viewpoints. Once you start thinking about listening in these terms, you'll never think of it the same way again.

Taking Listening in a New Direction

In a sense, we have shared in this book—you and I—a special kind of journey: a journey from listening obscurity to listening prominence and power. To put it another way, we have together gone from passive to active to influential listening. And what has sparked this entire venture is the fact that genuine dialogue has rarely before seemed so desirable and so elusive.

Moving forward, the larger questions are these: Are listeners to remain limited, silent partners at the margin of conversation? Or are listeners to realize their pivotal, natural role as conversational facilitators and influencers? Tradition suggests the former. Pragmatism suggests the latter.

That is the mission that calls to us today, defining our task and assuring us that, with persistence, we will be equal to it.

CHAPTER 10

The Seven Core Attributes of a Listening Leader

We are now in a position to appreciate the essential qualities that distinguish a true listening leader. As suggested when we began, these defining traits may be summarized in the form of an acronym spelling the word **P-R-E-S-E-N-T** (as in fully present). They are as follows:

P Listening leaders make *proactive participation* a *priority*. Thus they are able to forge genuine, strong *partnerships* with their conversational companions.

R They systematically *review* incoming information on-the-spot—through restatement and afterward—and are therefore in a better position to retain and retrieve vital information.

E Savvy listeners are *empathetic* listeners. They not only think along with their partners but also *feel* along with them, registering expressed emotions on their personal Richter scale.

S *Star events* are sidestepped. Articulate listeners know to expect occasional negative or belittling remarks (mental potholes) in conversation and counteract their provocativeness (emotional turbulence) by weighing in with a bit more questioning or other forms of response.

E Such high-performing listeners are proactive—not reactive. They make a conscious *effort* to pay attention and take matters of focus and responding into their own hands (average listeners pay their respects).

They don't rely on the subject's interest or the speaker's quality to draw their listening.

N Although we have every right to evaluate a speaker's presentation and message, these listeners hold back just a bit to *neutralize* snap judgments in the interest of gaining a fuller hearing and making a more objective assessment.

T Finally, the true listening leader *tenaciously* tracks both the speaker and the message, with high commitment to taking the full measure of the message (both substance and mood).

Functions of Feedback

We have seen that listening leads a double life. It has a *comprehending function*, by which we try to absorb what someone is telling us and understand its meaning. It also has a relationship, or *communicative function*, whereby to some degree we need to connect with the speaker. This is where most of us come up short. However—and this is really the key point—it is precisely here where we can have the strongest impact in our transactions with others.

At various times throughout our discussion, we have mentioned feedback and response and their beneficial work in conversations. Now we bring them together in a comprehensive summary to help the reader see the overall picture and refer to it as needed.

Feedback has much more dimension and more benefit than the act of responding implies. Listeners need to rediscover the strategic importance and appeal of feedback and how to give it. But we have noted that, like an anticipated report that's not out yet, feedback seems to be perpetually pending. Many seem to operate with feedback as though it is a gift, a dispensation bestowed seldom and randomly. Little or no feedback (negative publicity) may not be intended as hurtful behavior, but it is unsupportive behavior. In the absence of feedback, typically one of two things happens: either talk remains at a polite and superficial level, or the conversation never quite gets going. It depends on genuine responsiveness to see it through.

Here are some ways that listener feedback benefits the speaker, the listener, and the conversational relationship:

How Feedback Works for the Speaker

- Avoids a keep-you-guessing style by making the listener more knowable, quashing the speaker's doubts about his or her partner's listening health
- Implicitly ratifies the value of what is said
- Improves the speaker's concentration and fine-tunes his or her thinking
- Keeps the speaker posted on whether the listener understands and to what degree
- Increases the speaker's message value by improving its quality—whether in terms of more animated delivery, greater focus, precision, expansion, or confirmation
- Engenders a higher level of confidence and self-regard

How Feedback Works for the Listener

- Increases listener credibility by bringing humanity to this role
- Tames the tendency to drift by grounding obsessive mind wandering in the moment
- Gives attention a fresh start
- Allows for joint ownership of the transaction, as the speaker's message also becomes the acknowledged property of the listener
- Improves listener focus by helping the speaker, in turn, bring more interest, focus, precision, expansion, or confirmation to the message
- Provides the listener a richer and fuller context in which to understand and interpret what is said
- Helps keep a listener's emotional engines from overheating by dissipating the turmoil caused by star events
- Leads to a more stress-free listening style
- Engenders in the listener a higher level of confidence and self-regard

How Feedback Works for the Conversation

- By turning static, one-way reception into dynamic dialogue, it helps bridge the divide sometimes separating speaker and listener
- Achieves a more trustful relationship
- Gives direction and momentum to conversation, sustaining its forward movement
- Allows for the discovery of common ground
- Keeps the conversation on center
- Achieves mutual goals more easily by defining the transaction as a more efficient and productive encounter between equals

When we give responsiveness and feedback a more generous place among our communication concerns, we unleash a power that deepens every aspect of conversation. Listening to one's partner in this way becomes an art and craft as active and influential as talk itself. Far from invalidating the speaker–listener contract, sensitive and well-timed feedback affirms it. And, depending upon the situation, this may be the most important contribution a listener can offer.

APPENDIX 2

Thirteen Keys to Articulate Listening

We have seen that average listening efficiency is only about 25 percent, if that. The following keys help to increase concentration, memory, and rapport.

1. Understand that listening is a powerful influencing skill.
2. Distinguish between hearing (physical process) and listening (mind process).
3. Take responsibility for listening. Don't depend on the speaker.
4. Control major causes of poor listening: distraction, distortion, and defensiveness.
5. Delay judgments: size the speaker and subject up thoughtfully.
6. Slow down. The brain works three to four times faster than people speak. Interpret, evaluate....
7. Use a direct eye—face orientation. Make the speaker your primary focus.
8. Identify and neutralize emotional expressions (star events) that may sidetrack your thinking.
9. Curb the urge to jump in. Hear people out in order to absorb accurately and to be perceived as sincere.
10. Connect with the speaker by paraphrasing content, to verify and clarify meaning; responding, to signal understanding; taking notes,

to show interest and increase recall; asking questions, to understand; and reflecting feelings and implications, to develop rapport and trust.

11. Pause to listen between the lines.

12. Recall by association (personal experience), review (keep fresh), written references, visualizing (mental picture), repeated use (names), and abbreviations or mnemonics (memory devices).

13. Practice becoming a more articulate listener. Save time, preserve information, and enjoy closer relationships.

Resources

Baker, Larry, and Kitty Watson. *Listen Up: How to Improve Relationships, Reduce Stress, and Be More Productive by Using the Power of Listening.* New York: Three Rivers Press (member of the Crown Publishing Group, a division of Random House), 2000.

Barrett, Deborah. *Leadership Communication.* New York: McGraw-Hill/Irwin, 2005.

Bell, Chip R. *Managers As Mentors: Building Partners for Learning.* 2d ed. San Francisco: Berrett-Koehler, 2002.

Business Listening Web site. http://www.businesslistening.com.

Chowdhury, Subir. *The Power of Six Sigma.* Chicago: Dearborn Trade, 2001.

Covey, Stephen. *The Seven Habits of Highly Effective People.* New York: Fireside (Simon & Schuster), 1989, 2000.

Dana, Daniel. *Conflict Resolution.* New York: McGraw-Hill, 2001.

Gladwell, Malcolm. *The Tipping Point, How Little Things Can Make a Big Difference.* Boston: Little, Brown, 2000, 2002.

Glen, Paul. *Leading Geeks: How to Manage and Lead People Who Deliver Technology.* San Francisco: Jossey Bass Pfeiffer, 2002.

Goleman, Daniel, Richard Boyatzis, and Annie McKee. *Primal Leadership: Realizing the Power of Emotional Intelligence.* Cambridge, MA: Harvard Business School Press, 2002.

Holtz, Shel. *Corporate Conversations: A Guide to Crafting Effective and Appropriate Internal Communications.* New York: AMACOM, 2003.

International Institute for Listening Leaders Web site. http://www.listening leaders.com.

Kahane, Adam. *Solving Tough Problems: An Open Way of Talking, Listening, and Creating New Realities.* San Francisco: Berrett-Koehler, 2004.

Kelley, Tom, with Jonathan Litman. *The Art of Innovation: Lessons in Creativity from IDEO, America's Leading Design Firm.* New York: Currency (Doubleday), 2001.

Kouzes, James M. *The Leadership Challenge.* 3d ed. Hoboken, NJ: John Wiley, 2003.

Tannen, Deborah. *The Argument Culture: Moving from Debate to Dialogue.* New York: Random House, 1998.

Thull, Jeff. *Mastering the Complex Sale: How to Compete and Win When the Stakes Are High.* Hoboken, NJ: John Wiley, 2003.

Index

About the Author

Richard M. Harris, Ph.D., is president and founder of Richard M. Harris Associates, a nationally respected consulting firm specializing in business communication. With a client list that includes such Fortune 500 companies as Toys "R" Us, Fleet Financial Group, Johnson & Johnson, Gillette, Marriott, Staples, and IBM, he conducts customized workshops on speaking, listening, and presentation skills around the country. His articles on effective communication have been published in such journals as *Training and Development*, *Corporate Meetings & Incentives*, and *Financial Executive*. He lives with his wife in Teaneck, New Jersey.

To learn more about his distinctive training philosophy, rigorous methods, and programs in communicational leadership, visit his Web site at http://www.rmharrisassociates.com.